HIGH-RISK CHILDREN
IN SCHOOLS

HIGH-RISK CHILDREN IN SCHOOLS

Constructing Sustaining Relationships

Robert C. Pianta
and
Daniel J. Walsh

Routledge / New York & London

Published in 1996 by
Routledge
29 West 35 Street
New York, NY 10001

Routledge
11 New Fetter Lane
London EC4P 4EE

**Library of Congress Cataloging-in-Publication Data
available from the Library of Congress.**

To our children:
Meghan, Tony, Timmy, Scooter, and Buck

Contents

Preface

Both of us have spent our adult lives working directly and indirectly with young children who, for various reasons, have been marginalized by society. We started our careers as public school teachers, Pianta as a middle-school special-education teacher in New Britain and Bloomfield, Connecticut, and Walsh as a preschool and kindergarten teacher in the inner city of Chicago (with two brief interludes in San Diego and San Francisco). We still consult with and work directly in school-based programs for young children.

For the past eight years, as university researchers, we have been involved extensively with public schools' attempts to deal with the increasing number of children having difficulties in school. Pianta developed a screening program that blends measures of developmental abilities with measures of the life context of children entering kindergarten in Charlottesville, Virginia, and has an interest in the relationships children form with teachers. Walsh worked closely with the early-childhood teachers in the Albemarle County, Virginia, schools for many years and with the Washington Early Childhood Program in Urbana, Illinois. Coincidentally, as we finish this, we both have children in public schools—daughters in fourth grade, and Pianta also has a son in second grade.

We write with a firm conviction that schools can make an important and beneficial difference in the lives of young children, but we remain equally convinced that schools are not in fact making that difference with those children now being labeled "at risk." This is why we undertook writing this book, which is truly a collaborative venture. Walsh brought to this project the vision and perspective of an anthropologist. He appreciates qualitative design and data, sees the effects of culture and context, and has a rich and varied set of experiences in the public schools. Pianta is schooled in social development and in psychopathology. He comes from a more quantitative research tradition and works with children from various clinically identified groups. Both of us have a great appreciation for social processes and their role in development and schooling. We continue to be active participants in the schooling of young children as consultants to a range of settings that try to address risk through schooling.

Writing this book took much longer than we originally anticipated;

it required many trips back and forth between Illinois and Virginia. One reason for the longer schedule is that we both worked on all of it. Most of the book has been written by one, and rewritten by the other. On more than one occasion, we have been unable to identify the originator of an idea.

We would not have finished this book without the support of family and colleagues. Bob McNergney and the Commonwealth Center for Research on Teaching provided support for the trips between Illinois and Charlottesville, and played a role in getting us together to think about and work on the ideas in this book. Walsh extends thanks to Hui-Ling Su and Kyunghwa Lee for their help in proofing, Xiaohui Wang for the tedious job of checking the references, and the participants in the spring 1995 post-Piagetian perspectives seminar for their feedback and ideas. Pianta appreciates the contributions of Jeanne Stovall for preparation of figures and general help in producing the manuscript; Arnold Sameroff, Alan Sroufe, and Herb Leiderman, faculty of the Human Development and Psychopathology seminar at the Center for Advanced Study in the Behavioral Sciences for providing a better understanding of systems theory and development, and the University of Minnesota Institute of Child Development, where much of the writing took place. Byron Egeland provided access to the data archives of the Minnesota Mother-Child Interaction Study, which educated Pianta about social context, risk, and complexity.

We also thank our wives and children. They put up with our absences from home while we traveled to finish this book. They endured revisions, slow progress, and the many hassles that derive from bringing a project to completion. Finally, they educated us about development and systems in ways that brought meaning to theory.

Robert C. Pianta and Daniel J. Walsh

Introduction

We begin with the conviction that those children who are labeled as "at risk" are not well served by this society and its schools. At a time when 24% of all children under six and 59% of children under six in single-mother families live in poverty, when 60% of all poor children are minorities (National Center for Children in Poverty, 1993), and when poverty is but one of the many hazards that children in contemporary society face, we must be concerned about these children's future because they are society's future. The solution does not lie in massive restructuring of schools. More important than how schools look is how educators look at the children who enter the schools each day and how educators see their roles in those children's lives. To facilitate change in how to look at children we present a theoretical perspective for understanding the contemporary realities in which schooling and children are embedded—a perspective we call the Contextual Systems Model (CSM).

The efforts of a very large number of people and large amounts of money are spent in the endeavor of educating "at-risk" children. Unfortunately, this endeavor has had little in the way of a theoretical base from which to work. Hence many of the efforts and dollars expended to improve this situation are not well-informed. This is of great concern in an era of accountability and budget-cutting in education and social policy.

The burgeoning population of children characterized as "at risk" presents the most formidable challenge facing public education in the United States. This group of children "fails" in school largely because the relationship they have with schooling has deteriorated and attempts to fix it have been narrow, reflexive, and reactive. New perspectives on this problem are needed. This book uses insights from systems theory and developmental psychology to present a theoretical framework for the study and education of young children who are highly likely to fail at formal schooling.

Systems theory is widely accepted in many areas of the behavioral sciences, but it has not yet penetrated discourse on the education of young children. Furthermore, although there is a considerable amount of literature on "at-risk" children, it is primarily focused on middle- and high-school children and the problems of dropping-out and risk-taking behaviors. There really is no systematic, theoretically based literature on education and risk in the early grades. This volume is intended to fill this gap.

The book focuses on explaining the relationships between the child and other systems: family, community, culture, and most important, school. Current discourse on "at-risk" children is simplified by reductionistic approaches to the problem. Theory tends to identify the "problem" as being in one of three places: the child, the family, or the school. The Contextual Systems Model moves toward a perspective through which the problem of failure in the early grades can be viewed more comprehensively, emphasizing established links to developmental psychology. This model emphasizes systems, particularly school, as contexts for development.

In critiquing reductionistic perspectives, we offer constructs from General Systems Theory as an alternative. Specifically, General Systems Theory is applied to the problems of educating children who live in very high-risk situations, and the concept of risk is broadened and applied in systems terms. The Contextual Systems Model of risk and schooling in the early grades brings a fresh perspective to discourse on early schooling and risk, and has implications for training, policy, and practice. Detailed discussions are provided on the concept of risk and General Systems Theory principles as applied to (1) risk, (2) the education of young children, (3) child development, and (4) life hazards producing risk. The presentation is enhanced with several cases of actual children, entering the early grades under high-risk circumstances. Case-based information is linked with the principles of systems theory. Finally, school and schooling in the early grades are discussed with reference to the model presented, and the discussion is brought to a close with implications of the model for research, training, policy, and practice. In short, the book offers a viable method for educators to view and discuss children whose risk for academic and other failure is unacceptably high, a method that will not lead to the restructuring of schools by itself, but will redefine the relationship between schooling and families.

GOALS

Lee Chronbach argued that it is the "special task of the social scientist in each generation to pin down contemporary facts...[and] to realign culture's view of [people] with present realities" (1975, p. 126). But in order to do this we have to have a theory. As no doubt many before us have said, nothing is more practical than a good theory. To quote from W. Edwards Deming, "Knowledge is prediction, and knowledge comes from theory. Experience teaches nothing without theory" (cited in Glasser, 1993, p. xi). Theory is what is missing in the contemporary discourse on risk. Theory offers a coherent explanation of how part of the world works; it leads us to understand that part of the world in a way that makes it manageable. Good theory allows us to see contemporary reality through contemporary lenses rather than through the lenses used yesterday. Most important, for those of us working in applied fields, a good theory points us toward action.

Society is more complex today than it was 10 or 100 years ago, and ways of thinking about children and society must mirror that complexity. For example, children need more sophisticated skills to succeed today than did their parents or grandparents. The high-school drop-out rate has been stable for decades (Whelage, Rutter, Smith, Lesko, & Fernandez, 1988), but dropouts were once absorbed into a manufacturing economy. They no longer are. The rise of advanced technologies, and their increasing prominence in the home and the workplace, will only increase the pool of "unabsorbed" workers. Human potential is being wasted. At the same time, society has become increasingly rigid and constrained for children. Children go from before-school programs to school to after-school programs. From a very early age many spend a majority of their waking hours in day care. As Tobin (1991) has pointed out, contemporary children are under almost continual surveillance. It is not that we should not know where our children are, but there is a difference between caring for children and stripping their privacy from them. The fact that children no longer have the once-assumed privacy of being able to go off with their friends or be alone unobserved for a few minutes or a few hours each day simply increases the rigidity of their lives. One might consider how different one's own childhood would have been had one been under constant surveillance.

Contemporary realities are complex; large numbers of children are increasingly identified as failures, and schooling seems not to play a role in stemming those failures. It is our goal, in writing this book, to "pin down" contemporary reality with respect to marginalized children labeled "at risk" and to realign the view of that reality using the Contextual Systems Model. As a lens on the realities of risk, CSM embraces complexity, probability, and uncertainty, action and inter-action. Most lenses applied to risk tend to simplify, embracing linear causality and static categorization of problems.

To the extent that the complex behavior of complex living systems can be understood, that understanding will have, as Cronbach argued, a very short half-life, but without theory we are not going to arrive at a better understanding of the relationship between schools and chil-dren. We will not understand how educators perceive children and interact with them, and what factors affect these perceptions and inter-actions. We will not understand how children (and families) perceive schools and schooling, how they interact with and in schools, and what factors affect this process. Most important, we will not under-stand how both sides come together to form a relationship.

We do not think the answer lies in focusing attention on either side of this relationship between children and schools—it cannot be reduced to getting children ready for school, or to getting schools ready for children. There is no state of "readiness" that either children or schools can achieve that will guarantee a fit for all children in all schools. Rather the answer lies in where and how children (and fam-ilies) and schooling come together in a relationship, and in the quali-ty of that relationship. Our goal is to advance understanding of how to optimize this relationship. This book has simple and straightforward goals. We seek to provide a way of viewing children and schooling that results in schools that are more caring and flexible, in which there are many routes to success.

As social systems, schools must become increasingly flexible, and if schools are to meet the needs of contemporary children, they must become less formal. At the same time they must be intellectual. Children who depend on schooling for all their formal education must be challenged and nurtured intellectually beyond what their more for-tunate peers may require. What they do not have access to in schools, they are unlikely to have access to elsewhere. Socially rigid and narrowly academic schools will serve neither our children nor us well. It is our firm belief that a feasible way of understanding the complexity of contemporary life is required before we will be able to deal practically with realities that these high-risk children and the schools to which they come face day in and day out.

OVERVIEW OF THE BOOK

The book is divided into three sections. Part One consists of three chapters that describe risk from current demographic and theoretical bases. Chapter 1 provides a demographic snapshot of the realities of children's lives that undermine education and development. These are the "givens" that any consideration of schooling must address. The chapter introduces formal concepts regarding risk, the nature of risk, and risk research that are used throughout the book. In chapter 2 the main focus is on several dominant discourses that have been used to explain risk and schooling—political discourse, the readiness debate, and Piagetian theory. Chapter 3 introduces the concept of relationship as it applies to the association among children and families and schooling, and critiques theoretical models that locate risk in the child, in the family, or in the school.

Part Two begins with a chapter presenting the Contextual Systems Model as a new lens for examining risk and schooling, followed by chapters extending the discussion of CSM in terms of General Systems Theory, applications to schooling, developmental processes, and the life circumstances faced by children living under risk conditions. Chapter 4 builds on the previous introductory chapters and presents the Contextual Systems Model for discussing the relationship between children and families and schooling. This framework is grounded in systems theory, and systems perspectives on the relationship aspects of this association are discussed in detail.

Understanding risk and schooling is challenging in part because the realities are so complex. Chapter 5 builds on the previous chapters by formally introducing the concepts of General Systems Theory that are applied in the model presented earlier. These concepts are defined, and examples are used that specifically relate these concepts and CSM to "problems" in the education of "at-risk" children. The chapter formally critiques many existing applied and research approaches that fail to reflect the complexity of contemporary realities.

The Contextual Systems Model heavily emphasizes a developmental perspective for understanding risk. Development is understood as primarily a function of interactions taking place between child and context. Therefore, chapter 6 focuses exclusively on the child (from birth to age eight) and the systems theory principles governing developmental processes in this period. The principles link to the previous chapters and are specifically tied to educational procedures with high-risk children (e.g., assessment). Chapter 7 then turns to a more detailed discussion of contextual influences on development, in particular those that contribute to risk. These influences, termed "life hazards" are the contexts in which development occurs prior to entering school. Chapter 7 builds on earlier notions of risk as a property of systems, provides a discussion of the factors associated with risk, and reviews research on the consequences for development of exposure to selected forms of life hazards. Again, a systems perspective is used to provide an explanation for interrelationships among hazards, and the manner in which they affect development.

The book concludes with Part Three, which contains two chapters that use the Contextual Systems Model to focus on schooling. Chapter 8 describes schooling in the comptemporary society, examining schools as systems, as contexts for development, or as enhancers and intensifiers of risk. Chapter 9 directly addresses educational problems and implications for practice, policy, and research.

Throughout the book case descriptions of children with high-risk coefficients are presented. These case illustrations are intended to ground the concepts presented in the narrative in the real-life experiences of children as they develop in early childhood and enter school. These cases serve as way to frame the theory and conceptual models presented.

AN EXAMPLE OF CONTEMPORARY REALITY

We do not use the term "at-risk" children in this volume because of its vagueness. However, the book is concerned with children whose probability of failure in school and life is high, unacceptably high. These children are sometimes referred to as the "bottom 20%," although as social movement in our society appears to be moving more rapidly downward than upward, the bottom 20% may soon become the bottom 25% or more (Li & Bennett, 1994). These children, given their contemporary realities, will not succeed in school, unless those realities are somehow changed or made more manageable. The following case study describes life circumstances of a young six-year-old child. As will be demonstrated in a later chapter, the life circumstances of this young girl are all too common in contemporary America.

Case Study: *Sara*

Sara is the fourth of six children. This case could be written about any of the six, as their life stories are almost identical. Sara's mother and father both have a high-school education. Mother, father, and children live in a three-bedroom house in an established, suburban neighborhood with maternal grandparents and an uncle who is 31. Sara's father has been intermittently employed for the past ten years, but most of the time he has been unemployed. Her mother works 40–60 hours a week in an office. Sara is a healthy six-year-old child who does not know the alphabet. Like her four sisters, she enjoys playing with younger children but has no friends. No children from outside the family have ever been invited to Sara's house.

Sara and her siblings spend their days going to school, then either going to day care or coming home. When they are home, the children play outside throughout the neighborhood; there are almost never any adults playing with them. Sara and her siblings are frequently lost in the neighborhood, and often they are gone for several hours before any adult notices their absence.

One day, Sara rode the bus home from school with a friend. She invited herself for dinner, and by the friend's mother's report, ate a considerable amount of food for a child her age, then at 7 p.m. (it was dark) decided she would walk the four blocks home. The friend's mother drove Sara home, and Sara's father reported that he was beginning to wonder what had happened to Sara. There are almost no regular routines in Sara's household. Children eat when they want and what they want. Bedtimes are between 9 and 10 p.m. and 4–5 children sleep in a room. Discipline comes in the form of a threat by the father to use the belt or a gruff yell and spanking by the mother.

There is little or no affection shown to these children. Sara's parents show up for conferences, school activities, and occasionally Parent-Teacher Association (PTA) meetings. They appear interested in her progress and always nod willingly when teachers talk to them about things they can do at home. Sara is neglected by almost every standard except a legal one. School personnel "know" this family yet referrals to Child Protection are unfounded, and there are no programs that reach this family's needs. Sara is far behind on all measures of "preacademic" progress, and although she is a warm, caring, and enjoyable child, she is falling further and further behind.

Many questions follow from such a description. What is the nature of Sara's risk? What is her prognosis? What will be the pathway of her development from kindergarten through high school? Who or what is responsible for Sara? How are home and school connected in Sara's life?

Sara's brief story suggests the complex nature of risk and the many ways in which schooling interacts with the child/family system to produce poor school outcomes. One could easily argue that even without school being a factor in Sara's life, her risk for mental health or developmental problems is very high. The introduction of school and its own set of demands and challenges also introduces new sources of risk (or resource) into the developmental system that is the child. The challenge to educators is to first understand the nature of risk and then to appreciate the ways in which school interacts with risk and with aspects of the child/family system that also offer resources for development. In this way the school has the potential for becoming a resource and context for development itself.

part one
Risk

1

Contemporary Children and Risk

In this chapter we first provide a demographic snapshot of the realities facing contemporary children. We then introduce perspectives on the use of the term *risk* to describe children immersed in these realities. Finally we present a metaphor for risk.

A demographic picture of children and families in contemporary America begins to describe the appalling contexts of development that are at least tolerated and perhaps accepted in our society. This picture reflects a downward trend over the past 20 years, reflecting Moynihan's (1993) contention that deviance (here operationalized in terms of a society's tolerance for poor living conditions for its children) has been "defined down." In other words, former examples of deviance become tolerated and accepted by the culture while even more extreme forms of deviance emerge. These are the conditions under which children are educated in the United States. They stand as a formidable challenge to the notion that all children will be ready, however one perceives readiness, for school by the year 2000. Their complexity reveals the underlying need for conceptual models capable of integrating information on sources and levels of risk. Any comprehensive conceptual framework must first start with these factors as "givens" that must somehow be accommodated in discussing the relationship between children and families, and schooling.

DEMOGRAPHICS OF RISK: LEVELS AND SOURCES OF NEED

When we wrote this section of the book we debated about the extent to which statistics and figures reflecting social problems should be introduced into the book and where. It seems that every issue of any major newspaper or national magazine contains articles that describe a litany of social pathologies, many of which involve children, families, and schools. We use these data as a backdrop, as a frame for looking at children, families, and schooling, and as a stark reminder of the urgency of the situation. Most of these demographic data are based on the 1990 census. Unless otherwise noted, statistics come from Children's Defense Fund publications.

Each year the Fordham Institute for Innovation in Social Policy publishes the *Index of Social Health*, which it describes as

> A method of monitoring the social well-being of American Society. It is similar to the Consumer-Price Index, the Gross National Product, or the Dow Jones Average, but instead of measuring the movement of the economy or the stock market, the Index of Social Health measures the country's progress in addressing its major social problems. (1992, p. 2)

The 1992 Index reported on 1990 as having the lowest rating in 21 years. Nine of the 16 social problems rated (e.g., infant mortality, drug abuse, unemployment, homicide) grew worse, three improved, and four remained about the same. Of the nine problems that worsened, six reached their *worst recorded level*. These included child abuse, teen suicide, health insurance coverage, average weekly earnings, out-of-pocket health costs for those over 65, and the gap between the rich and the poor (Fordham Institute for Innovation in Social Policy, 1992).

In the spring of 1994, the Carnegie Commission (Young, 1994) issued a report on the development of young children in relation to schooling and other social outcomes. This report, a compilation of the work not only of educators but of a wide range of disciplines, concluded that by age three most of the life experiences necessary for supporting adequate development had to be in place in order for a child to make use of subsequent exposure to school and community resources, and that it was more than apparent that a large segment of the population lacked these basic components of "developmental infrastructure." Consequently, more and more children were growing up in seriously compromised circumstances that affected brain development, cognition, learning, and socialization. The scope and urgency of this report was unprecedented, as was the emphasis on the period from birth to age three as a *necessary* building block for later competencies. No longer was the problem of increased school failure rates located in the K–12 period. Instead a clear developmental emphasis was used to underscore the links between early experience prior to and often out of school, and subsequent experience in school. Following are some of the conditions that gave rise to the Carnegie Commission conclusions.

In 1991 economic, social, and political conditions combined to form a large group of poor Americans than had been seen in the previous 20 years (Greenstein, 1992). In 1992, 26% of all children under the age of six were poor, up from 17.7% in 1976 (Li & Bennett, 1994; Strawn, 1992). In 32 states the poorest fifth of families grew poorer in the 1980s and the purchasing power of the maximum Aid for Families with Dependent Children (AFDC) benefit for a family of three declined 43% in the median state, reflecting a benefit loss of more than $3,400 a year (in constant 1992 dollars). Between 1987 and 1992 the number of poor children under six grew from 5 to 6 million (Li & Bennett, 1994). In 1992 half of the 17.2 million children living in one-parent families were poor. The *average* black child spends 5.5 years in poverty between ages 4 and 18. Yet two-thirds of all poor children are white.

Emphasizing the linkages among risk factors, Duncan (1991) reported three major reasons for the increase in children's poverty from 1970 to the late 1980s: changes in family structure, particularly the increasing numbers of mother-only families; changes in the labor market (low wages and unemployment); and reductions in government transfers such as AFDC.

Living circumstances also changed for children. Where and under what circumstances a child was housed is a fairly new risk factor in studies of child development (Masten, 1992). Between 1970 and 1989 children living in doubled-up households increased 42%, to almost 5 million children. Homelessness threatened an increasing number of children; a 1989 survey of 27 cities conducted by the U.S. Conference of Mayors reported that 1 of 4 homeless persons in cities is a child, and requests for shelter by families rose 29% from 1988 to 1989. Families with children are the fastest growing subgroup of the homeless, now estimated at approximately one-third of the overall population (Bassuk, 1989, p. 1). The U.S. Department of Education estimates that 220,000 school-aged children are homeless and that 65,000 of them do not attend school (Reed & Sautter, 1990). The General Accounting Office estimated that on any given night, 186,000 children who are not actually homeless are "precariously housed," living on the verge of homelessness. Furthermore, an estimated 407,000 children, up 50% from 1986, depend on an overwhelmed and inadequate foster-care system. The Department of Health and Human Services calculates that over the course of a year, as many as one million youngsters under age 18 lack a permanent home or live on the streets (Reed & Sautter, 1990). Many of these children come to school each day.

Children's health is one of the most efficient ways to index the level of risk to children in a given society or community because health statistics are fairly easy to measure and communicate, these statistics are very telling. The United States ranks 22nd in the world in preventing infant deaths (Shiono & Behrman, 1995). In 1991 the infant mortality rate was 8.9 in 1000 over all, but for black babies it was 17.6 in 1000. In in Washington DC the mortality rate for black babies was 26 in 1000. A black child born in inner-city Boston has less chance of surviving his or her first year than a child born in Panama, North Korea, or Uruguay. During the 1970s the proportion of mothers receiving late or no prenatal care improved 3.5% a year; during the 1980s it worsened 2.5% a year. Twenty-five percent of all U.S. infants receive no early prenatal care early; 40% of black and Hispanic infants lacked such care. The National Center for Health Statistics and Westat published a *Children's Health Index* (1993) that lists the percentage of infants born in 1990 in the United States with one or more of six health risks. In 1993, 45% of all U.S. births involved one or more risk factors. The United States ranks 17th in polio immunizations, and 55th in nonwhite polio immunizations. In 1990 there were 27,000 cases of measles, which resulted in 90 deaths. The incidence of measles increased five times from 1988 to 1989 and ten times from 1983. Several infectious diseases associated with poverty—rheumatic fever, hemophilus influenza, meningitis, gastroenteritis, and parasitic diseases—are on the rise.

What happens to children exposed to these risks? For an increasing number of children the future holds not only academic failure, but many other failures as well—alienation, dysphoria, and violent death. In 1988, 1.8 million teenagers were the victims of violent crime. The suicide rate for teenagers between 15 and 19 more than tripled between 1960 and 1988. Suicide is now the third leading cause of death for 15 to 27-year-olds, behind motor vehicle accidents and homicide. The leading cause of death among black males 15 to 19 years old is murder as a result of a gunshot-wound; the homicide rate for young black males rose 43% from 1987 to 1990, up to 130.5 per 100,000 (Public Health Service, 1992). Between 1975 and 1986 the percentage of poor high-school graduates aged 18 to 20 who were attending college dropped from 34% to 30%. In contrast, students from well-educated affluent families were six times more likely to graduate from college within six years as were students from families with fewer resources.

To complete an intergenerational cycle, twice as many teens in the United States as in other industrialized countries have babies. One million get pregnant annually; half have babies, and half of these do not receive early prenatal care. One in four mothers having her first baby in 1988 was a teenager, and 65.9% of these teens were unmarried, compared to 33% in 1970. In Washington, DC, 94.7% of all teens giving birth are unmarried. At least 40,000 teens drop out of school each year due to pregnancy, and fewer than six of ten adolescent mothers graduate from high school by age 29. Regardless of race, teens who have below-average academic skills and are from poor families are about five to seven times more likely to have babies than teens with solid skills from nonpoor families.

How do children succeed against such a backdrop? What paths do their life courses take during the early school years? What happens to them in school? What kinds of friendships do they form? Does schooling have an effect on these children? How? What are the major influences on their lives? These are the issues and questions involving the nature of risk, the origins and course of school failure, and the actions schools can take to address the many levels and sources of need described previously. For many children the business of daily life has become very hazardous. The demographic statistics described above have real-life counterparts in children currently attending schools, children like those described in the brief case studies found at the end of each section of this book. It is little wonder that the major "risk factor" for most studies of children likely to develop behavioral, academic, health, or other problems is poverty.

At the same time, we do not wish to confound poverty, or race, with risk. To do so would be to ignore a huge, less-noticed population of more economically advantaged children whose development is compromised in other ways, mostly social and relational. Not lacking in physical resources, these are children whose relationship patterns have been stretched thin by family disruptions (e.g., divorce, separation) and other social conditions. These children also find their way into the "bottom third," although their high risk coefficients are not attributable to poverty. In any case, we call attention to the stark realities of children whose chances for school failure are unacceptably high.

HIGH-RISK CHILDREN IN THE SCHOOLS

Schools have tried to grapple with the realities of social pathology and social inequities for as long as they have existed. The realities described above are not all new to the United States, although the level of need and rate of exposure in the population is unprecedented. The increased numbers of children coming to school exposed to these dire circumstances, and the difficulty in educating them, is, in part, one of the conditions that gave rise to the initial "Nation at Risk" report that first called national attention to the demographic realities facing schools and the high failure rates associated with these realities. In this context, the notion of risk and at-risk children became a popular rallying point for drawing attention to the large numbers of children whose experience in and out of school was compromising their capacity to become functional members of society.

> The description of at-risk students and their families should be familiar. After all, it is almost 200 years old, and it remains today, as it was when it first appeared, a formula used by reformers to arouse the public to action.... For almost two centuries, poor children—often nonwhite and from other cultures—have been seen to pose a threat to the larger society because neither parents nor existing community institutions could control their unacceptable behavior. Fear of having to spend more for welfare payments and prisons drove public officials to compel attendance in schools as a solution to the problems of children we would today label "at risk." (Cuban, 1989, pp. 780–781)

Thus the term "at risk" has both a long history and a strong appeal. The term has potential for influencing discourse in ways that might be fruitful, although a more thorough understanding of the concept of risk is required. Currently, the term is used to describe almost any child having difficulty in school, or as a euphemistic replacement for more offensive labels (Reeves, 1988). Both uses are incorrect. Neither helps advance our understanding of contemporary children.

DEFINING RISK

Risk refers to an actuarial, or probabilistic, relation between one index, for example, poor academic skills, and the likelihood of attaining a given outcome of interest, such as dropping out of school, given specified conditions or factors (Hess, Wells, Prindle, Lippman, & Kaplan,

1987). Risk does not refer to a causal process or etiological relation, that is, where one thing causes another, although a risk factor may indeed be integral to etiological processes (Eaton, 1981). Instead, risk status is a way of describing the likelihood that a given individual will attain a specific outcome, given certain conditions. The concept of risk emphasizes the probabilistic relations between specific factors and identifiable outcomes instead of some, at best, ill-defined relation between diagnosis and treatment. Eaton (1981) defines a *risk factor* as any event, condition, or characteristic that increases the probability of the occurrence of an identified target outcome (e.g., mental disorder, heart attacks, school failure, school-age pregnancy). A pervasive issue in risk research and especially its application to education is an understanding of the relation and distinction between risk factors and etiological processes.

Assigning risk status to an individual means that he or she shares characteristics similar to a group in which there is a known probability of attaining a certain outcome that is greater than the probability in the general population. We note that assigning such a probability to an individual must be done cautiously. Even very high correlations between groups and specified factors have limited predictive value for the individual. For example, a group correlation of 0.5, which is seen as relatively high in the social and behavioral sciences, "will provide a standard error of prediction that is 86 percent of the error that would be obtained by completely ignoring the predictor variable and simply using the group mean...to predict the value [for the individual]" (Cziko, 1992, p. 11).

For example, children who have flunked a grade before grade six and who have below-average reading skills in grade six are more likely to drop out of high school than students who have not flunked and who have average or above reading skills in the six grade (Hess et al., 1987). Thus flunking before grade six is a risk factor for dropping out. Flunking a grade may or may not be a cause of dropping out; it is not necessary to establish this in order for the concept of risk to be applied. Nevertheless, one must be very cautious in making predictions about any individual child who fits this profile because the increased probability of dropping out (the *risk coefficient*) is a property of the group of children who flunk a grade before grade six, not any given individual in that group. Other factors or combinations of factors may be more influential, factors may affect one child more than another. Further, these general predictions about children dropping out do not take into account actions taken by the school or the child after the sixth grade. We cannot change the fact that a child has been retained, and obviously we need to understand what it is about being retained in elementary school that is related to dropping out later. But we can address a child's reading skills. One assumes, other things being equal, that a child whose reading skills improve from below average to average or above will be more likely to graduate from high school than he or she would have had his or her skills remained low, or perhaps even deteriorated. The main point here is that risk status is a group-level descriptor; it denotes a characteristic that an individual shares with a group (i.e., exposure to some risk factor), which increases the likelihood or rate of a certain problem outcome within the group. It says nothing about individual probabilities, does not denote cause, and does not account for the multiple pathways that each group member takes on the way to a given outcome.

Another key element of the concept of risk is the link between risk status and preventive intervention. Risk status should be viewed as an index of eligibility for preventive intervention. Pianta (1990) has described three forms of intervention in relation to risk status in schooling. These three forms differ with respect to scope and timing. Primary prevention consists of actions that are aimed at the entire population, without respect to risk status, and are delivered before the causal process underlying the problem outcome begins, for example, inoculating all children for certain diseases. The aim of such interventions is to eliminate the problem outcome in the population. Secondary prevention comprises interventions that are delivered to a particular group—a high-risk group—whose probability of attaining the problem outcome is elevated. The link between high-risk status and secondary prevention enables the intervention to be targeted more narrowly than for primary-prevention efforts. Prekindergarten programs for poor four-year-olds is an example of secondary prevention. Secondary prevention is delivered before the problem outcome is attained by the group members. Finally, tertiary prevention encompasses those interventions delivered after a problem outcome has been attained. These actions basically involve remediation of the effects of a problem outcome and are offered only to those individuals who have attained problem-outcome status. Special education or programs for children with certain disorders or disabilities are examples of tertiary prevention.

Despite a well-articulated language of risk, and widespread definitions of terms and links to different forms of interventions (frequently in the field of public health), educators have been notoriously inaccurate in their use of the term, and appear fundamentally to misunderstand its applications. Often the term "at risk" is used as a labeling device to describe individual children without specifying the outcome that they are likely to attain, that is, exactly for what is the child at risk? Educators are also ignorant of the wider conceptual context in which risk is used—the context of prevention.

Thus, in one study educators identified remedial programs (those that intervene after a child has a certain problem) as secondary-prevention programs. They also endorsed the term "at risk" as a useful label for children who had been retained in grade, that is, who had already failed. Although they accurately identified risk factors for early school failure, they did not believe the schools could have a role in ameliorating the risk created by these factors (Pianta & Nimetz, 1989).

To the extent that "at risk" remains simply another descriptor for the children of the poor, the term remains an invidious label that clouds discourse, masks contemporary realities, and obfuscates efforts to address these realities. The notion of risk represents an important change from earlier descriptors, like *deprived* or *disadvantaged*. Although one can certainly be more or less deprived or disadvantaged, the terms as used simply denoted certain groups—these people are deprived, these are not—without attention to degree of deprivation or disadvantage. For example, women in this (and most societies) have experienced a societal playing field that was less than level, but for some groups of women, for example, poor minority women, the field was considerably more tilted than for others.

Overuse of the term "at risk" can also mask important realities. When we label a child as at risk, we imply that the outcome we are concerned about, which is most often academic failure, has not yet occurred and, one hopes, with the right intervention can be averted. In fact, the failure may have already begun. We return to our weak-reading sixth grader who has flunked a grade. Despite the fact that the best predictor of academic achievement is previous academic achievement (Alexander & Entwistle, 1988), the fact is that children at every level of schooling get their acts together and transform themselves from poor students into very successful students. We suspect that many of us are very fortunate that our early academic records, for example, elementary and high-school grades, were not a factor when we entered the academic job market. Thus to the extent that "at risk" is a label instead of a mechanism that links children with interventions aimed at interrupting the risk-outcome relation, the term becomes a means of "writing off" a segment of the population.

The very notion of risk is meaningless by itself, that is to say that it makes no sense to label children or anyone at risk unless one specifies for what and the level of risk. It is absurd to argue that one group is at risk and another is not. We are all more or less at risk for certain outcomes, for example, dying within the next 24 hours—how high the risk depends a lot on the immediate conditions. The coefficient of risk changes as conditions change. The risk of being struck by lightning varies greatly depending on whether one lives in a region where electrical storms are common, whether one is standing in a field or sitting in a house, and whether an electrical storm is occurring at the moment. Similarly one's risk of not learning to read varies greatly depending on the extent to which one is read to at home, the extent to which one is familiar with the alphabet, how caring and knowledgeable one's teacher is, whether one is learning to read a language that one speaks fluently, whether the reading experience itself is meaningful, and so on. We find the notion of risk a useful construct with which to think about and design ways to interrupt the cycles of failure.

Some (Swadener, 1989; Swadener & Lubeck, 1994) have suggested replacing the label "at risk" with "at promise." We too are concerned with the invidious effects of labeling young children. We have encountered kindergarten teachers who refer to those children who have attended a prekindergarten intervention program as "at-risk" children. Thus, in a perverse turn of events, children who have attended programs designed to ameliorate their risk for academic failure find themselves labeled in an invidious way, which they might have avoided had they not attended the program. Still, we reject adamantly the perversely nominalist idea that problems can be solved by changing labels. Renaming a problem does not solve it or make it go away. For many children, risk is very real—their risk of school failure is very high. The notion of risk has heuristic value over the two centuries of labels used to describe "poor children—often nonwhite and from other cultures…seen to pose a threat to the larger society because neither parents nor existing community institutions could control their unacceptable behavior" (Cuban, 1989, p. 781). We advocate a sensible, sensitive, and constructive use of the term and related concepts.

Risk Research

Research on risk, and on the factors attenuating risk, has received considerable attention in recent years (Garmezy, 1984). In this research, the concept of risk has been a useful tool for inquiry into the etiology of the problem of interest, the prediction of disorder, the identification of "protective factors," and the translation of this information into early intervention and prevention programs. Risk research involves longitudinal study of children exposed to risk factors. Such study involves assessment of subsequent exposure to factors that increase or reduce risk, and the positive or negative outcome status attained by individuals in the group (Garmezy 1977).

The expansion of an empirical research base pointing to predictors of a number of failure outcomes (academic and social failure, drug abuse, dropping out, school-age pregnancy) has contributed to the scientific foundation (Cowen, 1980) on which to build prevention programs. Knowledge of the predictors of negative outcomes provides the empirical basis for early-identification efforts supporting primary- and secondary-prevention programs.

Risk research holds considerable promise for developing prevention and early-intervention strategies. Knowing the risk coefficients associated with differing risk factors, and the outcomes they predict, can only add to the information base used to make decisions about how to best utilize scarce resources. Furthermore, identifying children who do well despite their risk status, and understanding the factors distinguishing them from their peers who do not do well, facilitate the development of prevention and early-intervention strategies (Rutter, 1987). For example, Pianta, Steinberg, and Rollins (1995) corroborated a long-standing finding indicating that children who perform poorly on measures of underlying ability do poorly in school and are more likely to be retained. They also discovered, however, that within this group of "children at risk for retention" there were children with whom teachers could openly communicate about personal matters, and with whom the teacher shared a warm relationship; these children were not retained. Thus, these components of the relationship between a child and a teacher could reduce the risk coefficient of individuals within a high-risk category. Such factors are considered "protective factors" and form the basis of prevention efforts, including efforts to stabilize and extend contact between children and a given teacher.

Protective and Vulnerability Mechanisms

What is critical then, to risk-reducing efforts, is understanding variations in individuals' responses to risk factors. These variations suggest ways that the risk situation can be modified to produce positive and negative outcomes, that is, why some people cope well with particular hazards, whereas others do not. Rutter (1987) has termed these positive and negative responses to risk and hazards *protective* and *vulnerability* mechanisms, respectively.

For Rutter, protective mechanisms operate to ameliorate or reduce the reaction to risk factors that in ordinary circumstances lead to a negative outcome. A protective mechanism could be something as simple as a teacher spending extra time with a young child whom he or she knows is experiencing conflict at home. In contrast, vulnerability mechanisms intensify the reaction to risk factors and hazards and lead to poor outcomes. Vulnerability mechanisms can be compared to the concept of interactions between hazards (Sameroff & Seifer, 1984). When exposure to one life hazard leads to exposure to further hazards (such as divorce leading to loss of income), a vulnerability mechanism is present in the interaction between these hazards. A vulnerability mechanism could also come into play when a teacher criticizes a child for acting in ways quite appropriate in the child's home culture.

In Rutter's view, interrupting vulnerability mechanisms involves assessing not only stress exposure, but the capacity of the individual and system to respond adaptively to the hazard. Intervention can be seen as interrupting vulnerability mechanisms by promoting positive coping responses (e.g., social skill groups for children of divorce), or providing resources to stress-exposed individuals (supportive child-care services for single mothers who need to work).

Because schools too often provide services for children only on the basis of children's failure (Gartner & Lipsky, 1987), accurate understanding of the term risk and its linkage to secondary and primary prevention is essential to creating a context within schools that is accepting of prevention, and in which prevention efforts can be implemented. Otherwise, current beliefs about risk, reflecting the prevailing emphasis on remedial interventions (tertiary prevention) are likely to prevail.

Systems and Risk

Finally, risk cannot be understood as a static concept. Although the notion of compiling probabilities linking certain experiences with certain outcomes is appealing, and in fact is the bread and butter of the insurance industry, this is not likely to occur in education. In part this is because educators have not grappled with defining the outcomes in which they are most interested (both positive and negative). Witness the debate on President Clinton's Goals 2000. Establishing standards for performance—the things we want children to know and do in school and as a function of schooling—is not only not a reality, the very idea is under attack. Furthermore, because education is primarily an effort to induce change, there is a dynamic quality to the relations between what a child brings to school and what a school brings to a child, which continually alters the risk coefficient of individuals and groups. Unlike insurance companies that keep careful track of certain outcomes (death, illness, car accidents), and the relation of these to certain easily observable events (cholesterol levels, number of speeding tickets), and basically ignore individual efforts to alter the links between these (exercise, etc.); the education system poorly documents or defines outcomes, has little knowledge of the risk factors for these outcomes (and attendant probabilities), and is heavily invested in improving outcomes regardless of the level of risk.

In short, the concept of risk presents a formidable challenge to educators. The problem outcomes being debated are complex and interrelated. Can we think of discipline problems as independent of poor achievement? The factors predicting those problems—home environment, school environment, individual capacities—are countless and interrelated to some degree. Thus, the concept of risk, which in pure form seems so straightforward, is challenged by the realities of educating children. Within the system that is schooling, risk must be seen in terms of process.

Risk and its associated constructs are useful to the extent that they advance discourse that links the contemporary realities of children's lives with the experiences they are (or might be) offered in school. Thus probabilities of different forms of failure are associated with certain risk factors. These probabilities can be used to deploy resources aimed at unlinking risk factors and outcomes in order to lower the probabilities. Through research on protective factors and educational programs that emulate these protective mechanisms, educators can develop a prevention-oriented service delivery system (Pianta, 1990).

This is an enormously complicated enterprise, yet it is critical if some systematic progress is to be made in reducing the costly consequences of the demographic realities presented earlier. In the remainder of this book, our intention is to provide a model for addressing risk as well as the language needed to undertake such an enterprise. The model we advance, the Contextual Systems Model, rests heavily on general systems theory, developmental research, and cultural perspectives. Before we provide a detailed view of the Contextual Systems Model, we will identify ways in which other perspectives have failed to adequately address the difficulties high-risk children have in school.

A METAPHOR FOR RISK

We use the term *conversation* as a metaphor for interaction between systems over time. Conversation connotes the dynamic interplay between two actors reflective of the dynamic interplay between child/family and schooling systems. Using this metaphor, risk can be viewed as a communication problem—the conversation (patterns of interaction) of the child-family and schooling systems does not produce shared meaning. Instead, there is misunderstanding, "differences," blaming, conflict, labeling, and alienation, all terms that have been used to describe the failure of schools, children, or families in relation to educating in high-risk circumstances.

Children who derive meanings from home and school that are reinforcing to one another, that are consonant or congruent or conversant with one another, are those for whom the relationship between the child/family and schooling systems is functional—it works with respect to facilitating the child's development in school. These are children being educated in low-risk circumstances. On the other hand, there are children who derive meanings from home (or school) that lead to conflicting emotions, motivations or goals, meanings that are inconsistent or incongruent within the child/family and schooling relationship. These are children being educated in high-risk circumstances. And again, we must underscore the idea that this conversation is embedded in larger systems, and that risk is a distributed property of these systems.

The purpose of the Contextual Systems Model is to assist educators and children "to come to terms with the communication problem" (Bruner, 1990a, p. x), not by blaming, or locating the problem in one or more corners of what we describe in chapter 3 as the invidious triangle, or by disengaging and giving up because the issues are intractable. Instead, we must recognize the distributed nature of risk for what it is, and understand that risk is created where systems that are responsible for regulating child development converse and share a relationship, or fail to do so. Then there is literally a crack into which children fall. School failure is at its core caused by an inability or an unwillingness to communicate—a relationship problem. Interestingly, as Bruner noted further, teaching (the relationship between the teacher and the learner) can be well characterized as "an extension of conversation" (Bruner, 1990a, p. x).

We do not mean to trivialize schooling or the process of learning by referring to it as conversation. Instead, our intention is to raise communication, and its daily enactment, conversation, to the level of complexity and sophistication it deserves, and to embed it within the factors that regulate its enactment. To see schooling as communication forces us to see its interactional or transactional (Bruner, 1987) nature, and to see it as conversation requires us to attend to all parties involved. To the extent that schooling has been and remains a monologue, the potential for failure for many of the children entering its world remains high. To the extent that meaning is not shared within a relationship, the relationship cannot function. By stressing communication as concretely enacted in daily interactions between people, we are stressing the importance of relationships across systems and the process of refining and tuning conversation that gives rise to functional activity. There has been too much focus on interactions within systems, particularly within the system of school, and on fixing those interactions. That approach has gotten us nowhere and will take us nowhere. The question is: Will children be able to get into the conversation in a meaningful way?

2

The Discourse on Risk
and Early Schooling

Much of the research on risk has taken place at the secondary level and has focused on dropouts and ways of preventing dropping out of high school (e.g., Ekstrom, Goertz, Pollack, & Rock, 1986; Fine, 1986, 1991; Natriello, 1986; Natriello, Pallas, McDill, McPartland, & Royster, 1988; Whelage, et al., 1988). A theme that runs through this literature is that dropping out begins early in a child's school career. Rumberger wrote, "The significant influence of family background suggests that the tendency to drop out begins early in a student's life. Attempts to combat the problem should therefore be initiated at an early age as well" (1983, p. 211).

Beginning with Head Start in 1966, a great deal of money and effort has been put into intervening early in children's school lives. Longitudinal studies (e.g., Schorr, Both, & Copple, 1991) particularly those from the High/Scope Foundation (e.g., Schweinhart, Barnes, & Weikart, 1993) have shown that such intervention programs can, in fact, reduce the incidence of dropping out. So, from one perspective, why bother with new theories and perspectives when we can simply identify components of programs that "work" and replicate them in new settings with more children? The problems with this perspective (embodied by many "best practices" approaches) are two central illusions: (1) the criteria of "success" for many programs is narrow and illusory, and (2) replication is illusory as well.

With regard to the criteria of success, the illusions are easy to spot.

Our concerns in this book go beyond trying to keep children in school. Many children remain in school and even graduate, yet are still academic failures. As Fine and Rosenberg found, "Camouflaged by the 'dropout' hysteria are the facts that Black teens *with* a high school diploma suffer 54% unemployment" (1983, p. 270). Gormoran wrote of his study of tracking, "In most cases the difference in achievement between tracks exceeds the difference in achievement between students and dropouts, suggesting that cognitive school development is affected more by where one is in school than by whether or not one is in school" (1987, p. 135). Maeroff commented, "In big city after big city, minority students by the tens of thousands leave school each year—some as dropouts, some as graduates—utterly unprepared to participate in and contribute to a democratic society" (1988, p. 633).

Attempts to bring dropouts back into the mainstream by offering them alternative routes to graduation have also been less than successful. Cameron and Heckman (1993) studied the effect of high-school-equivalent degrees and concluded "that exam-certified high school equivalents are statistically indistinguishable in their labor market outcomes from high school dropouts.... Both anecdotal and empirical evidence suggests that employees and the military discount the GED" (pp. 43–44).

The second illusion concerns replication. It is an almost commonplace phenomenon to come across efforts at school reform that have been successes in one place, which when implemented in another, do not work as well (e.g., Sarason, 1991). This is not, as many argue, a function of the fidelity of the implementation to the original program, but a natural consequence of complex systems and the failure to recognize the multiple factors constraining behavior within systems.

If we learn anything from the vast dropout literature, it is that in order to understand this "problem," which emerges after several years in school, we must appreciate the pathways that lead to this problem from very early in life. Clearly, then, if we are to address risk, we must start at the beginning.

A RELATIONSHIP WITH SCHOOLING

We focus on the early years of the relationship between children and their families, and the process of formal public schooling in the United States. The patterns of interactions that constitute this relationship are not single movements at single moments, for example, the morning a child first steps on to the school bus for kindergarten. Rather, they are part of an ongoing process patterned over many years, involving many dimensions of a child's life. We will speak often of these interactions and the relationship they reflect. We emphasize at the outset that this relationship is continual, multidimensional, and constantly changing. A child does not leave home for school once that Monday morning in late August or early September when, as a five-year-old, he or she enters kindergarten. The child leaves home for school every morning, something of which any parent whose child does not like school is painfully aware. The child is received (for better or worse) into the classroom each day. The transition to school is not over, and the relationship between home and school is not fixed, once the child enters the school or even the classroom. The process is continual.

Children begin a relationship with schooling even before they attend formal schools or preschools. They learn about schooling from siblings and neighbors. Their parents are busy preparing them in better and worse ways or struggling to discover how to prepare them for the many classroom years ahead (Graue, 1993). Once in school children are active participants in this relationship until they exit formal schooling (by one or another means) many years later.

As developmentalists, we are most interested in the early aspects of this relationship because they exert considerable influence on the development of the relationship between home and schooling. Current research, although it views the relationship between children and families and schooling more narrowly than we do, clearly and unequivocally documents the importance of the early phases of this relationship for the success of young children in school. Alexander and Entwistle (1988), in their comprehensive study of the Baltimore City schools, emphasize that the trajectories of children's adaptation in school are fairly fixed by the time children reach the third grade. This means that the early school years can be thought of as a sensitive period (Bornstein, 1989) for developing the skills, knowledge, and attitudes critical for school success.

As a sensitive period, the early school years take on unique importance in establishing the developmental infrastructure on which later experience will build. Minor adjustments to the child's trajectory of adaptation in the early years of school can have major effects on the child's later path through school and life. We are not saying that trajectories cannot be altered or deflected later in the school career but that the efforts to alter them required later are necessarily more intensive, probably more difficult, and usually more expensive. Nor are we saying that because Alexander and Entwistle found the trajectories to be fixed by third grade that this is inevitable. Their research, like all research, describes only what *is*, given existing circumstances. It says little about what *can be*, given different circumstances.

A word about sensitive periods in development. Bornstein (1989) argues that sensitive periods have special meaning for development. They are periods in which certain capacities are formed that feed forward (Ford & Ford, 1987) into later competencies developed by the child. That is, the effect of developing (or not) these capacities is not necessarily evident within the sensitive period, but becomes increasingly evident later, as demands for performance that builds on these early capacities increase.

Furthermore, sensitive periods can be fragile. In systems-theory terms they are often periods in which a system is particularly open to new information or influences, or is characterized by disequilibrium—a system in flux. Depending on how well this process of input or flux is regulated (organized, protected, buffered, shielded), the eventual output can vary immensely regardless of the capacities of the system prior to this sensitive period. Very often, it is the set of relationships between a system and larger surrounding systems that provides this buffering, regulating, or protective function. The relationship between child and family, and formal schooling serves exactly this regulatory or buffering role with respect to the sensitive period of early schooling.

It is important, then, that we understand the early phases of the relationship between schooling and the child. Understanding of this or any topic begins with a framework for discussion. Because ultimately what we do reflects this framework and the ideas embedded in it, it is important that we begin by understanding how we talk about risk and early schooling.

DOMINANT DISCOURSES

We begin then by talking about talk, or more formally, discourse. We define discourse as what is being said, written, or thought about something in a given cultural-historical context. A discourse reflects a set of shared, or common, understandings about the critical dimensions of something and the ways in which it is organized. At any given time, the discourse on a topic is bounded in important ways by culture, history, and the influence of certain individuals and groups. A discourse is affected by the ideas supported by it and the availability of words to express those ideas. It can be viewed as what we say and think about something as well as *how* we say and think it. Further, a discourse is always bounded by what we do not say and what we do not think—perhaps because we are unable, perhaps because we dare not. It is the accessible and the acceptable bounded by the inaccessible and the unacceptable. For example, the discourse of feminism is very different now from 75 years ago, and very different in this culture than it is in Iran.

A *dominant* discourse is the proper or correct way to talk about a topic. For example, at one time the dominant discourse of education was heavily behavioristic. It was considered most appropriate to speak in terms of reinforcement and responses and behavioral objectives when discussing children's education. The discourse of early childhood education has been since the late 1960s primarily Piagetian. Thus, early childhood educators speak of stages and assimilation and accommodation when discussing how children learn in a preschool setting. Although both behaviorism and Piagetian theory focus on interactions between school contexts and children, both have been shown to be inadequate with respect to conceptualizing the relationship between children and schools. We assume the reader is familiar with criticisms of behaviorism. The inadequacies of Piagetian theory will be discussed below.

For the rest of this chapter we first explore and critique the dominant discourses on high-risk children and schooling. The first discourse is political; the others are educational.

The Politics of Risk and Readiness

In 1989 President Bush met with the nation's Governors at the University of Virginia. The Education Summit resulted in Six National Educational Goals to be reached by the year 2000. In 1994 Congress adopted and President Clinton enacted *Goals 2000: Educate America Act*. The first goal states, "By the year 2000 all children will start school ready to learn." These goals, which typify the prevalent political rhetoric, fail on at least two counts.

First, the authors betray a remarkable lack of awareness of contemporary realities facing children and families. The stresses and strains on children and families in the 1990s are overwhelmingly more powerful than reflected in this plan. Second, the document reinforces two common but ultimately invidious notions of readiness that impede efforts to improve contemporary schooling. First, the idea that readiness for school can be defined in terms of a circumscribed set of preacademic skills that can be easily taught and measured is naive. Second, that children are the locus of readiness (however defined) contradicts the large body of literature recognizing the role of context in producing whatever skills a child has or does not have (e.g., Bradley, Caldwell, & Rock, 1988).

On the whole, Goals 2000 embodies the "quick fix" approach that has plagued American public schooling from its inception. That politicians pander to their constituents by offering simple solutions to what are intractably complex societal problems should not surprise us. But such political rhetoric cannot be ignored or dismissed as unimportant. This rhetoric, with its presidential stamp of approval, moves us yet another step away from the realities that educators face daily.

One could hope that the authors of Goals 2000 had something more substantial in mind, that they envisioned that all children will come to school from adequate housing, traveling through neighborhoods that are safe, that they will be healthy and strong, and that their parents will have adequately paying jobs. However, the fundamental contribution of political discourse on risk and schooling, the simple solution, mitigates against bringing these realities to the foreground. Politicians will always be involved in the discourse on schooling, but as educators and developmentalists we cannot permit politicians to define the discourse. It is essential that we recognize political realities and understand schooling within the larger political context. The one positive outcome of the Bush and Clinton plans is that it may help us do just that.

Readiness for School

The focus on readiness in Goals 2000 invites an extended discussion. As Graue (1993) has shown in her study of kindergartens in three communities, readiness is a complex social construction that varies from community to community, located not in the heads of the children but in the heads of the adults who together form expectations for them. Graue describes very conflicting constructions of readiness.

The contemporary early childhood discourse on readiness has been dominated by these conflicting constructions. Early childhood education discourse defines readiness in terms of what children can and cannot do, but the engine behind their ability or inability is maturation cloaked in Piagetian constructivist terms. The environment comes into play in a negative way, that is, a disadvantaged background can cause maturational delays. Thus, children's "failure" in school is seen as a function of a "lack of readiness," and instruction is withheld or provided based on readiness indices, for example, performance on the *Gesell School Readiness Test* (e.g., Ellwein, Walsh, Eads, & Miller, 1991; Walsh, Baturka, & Smith, 1992). The emphasis on teaching children only what they are "ready" to learn has had unfortunate consequences. As Bruner (1966) has pointed out, readiness "is a mischievous half-truth...largely because it turns out that one teaches readiness or provides opportunities for its nurture, one does not simply wait for it" (p. 29). The almost phenomenal ability of some children to perform complex mathematics calculations in the absence of instruction in contrast with the equally poor performance of children despite instruction (Resnick, in press) highlights the uselessness of the concept of readiness, especially as it applies to decisions regarding instruction, at the same time emphasizing the locus of readiness (however defined) as residing in the relationship between child and context.

Behaviorist perspectives continue to influence discourse on readiness by suggesting that readiness can be decomposed, or reduced, to critical skills (knowing the alphabet, a specified list of color names, etc.), which in turn can be taught through direct instruction. The most well-known example of this approach was *DISTAR* (Bereiter & Engelmann, 1966), widely used in the 1960s and 1970s for teaching what were then called "disadvantaged" children.

Even within a maturationist perspective, behavioral paradigms drive the means by which readiness is assessed and decisions about children are made. That is, children's "readiness" is assessed using checklists of preacademic skills (Meisels, 1987); they are taught complex skills (e.g., reading) using skill sequences derived from task analysis, and their progress is evaluated with respect to mastery of these skills. Nonetheless when performance on the assessments or evaluations of progress falls below some criterion, the explanation for this "failure" often has little to do with the environment, and a lot to do with "maturity."

These strange bedfellows do little justice to the complexity of the processes that account for children's adjustment to school. Readiness is located neither in the child's "maturational clock" that regulates development nor in his or her behavioral repertoire. It cannot be indexed to chronological age nor to an isolated checklist of skills.

To argue that all children will be ready for school ignores the reality that conceptions of readiness vary between communities and are constantly changing within communities and their schools. One of us (DJW) lives in a community where ice skating is popular and where a rink is open 11 months of the year. One commonly sees three- and four-year-old children dashing about the ice. By five many are playing hockey, taking up figure skating, or speed skating. One suspects that in many communities children that age would not be seen as "ready" for such activities.

To define readiness as some set of skills, for example, being able to count to 20, recite the alphabet, and name some arbitrary list of shapes and colors, simply masks the fact that some children will, under this rubric, be more or less ready for school than others. How does the child who meets these requirements measure up to the one who can count to 100 and read *The Cat in the Hat* (Seuss, 1957)? Each day teachers face children with a wide and seemingly increasing range of skills and knowledge and attitudes. Drawing a line among them to mark the "ready" from the "not ready" is an activity rarely tied to the complex constraints on a child's performance, regardless of where the line is drawn or what conceptual base defines the distinction. Furthermore, unless we want to exclude from school *all* children who are not ready by these criteria, the reality facing educators is that a large, heterogeneous pool of children will arrive at school on the first day of kindergarten and each day after that.

The emphasis on readiness is a way of ignoring or avoiding dealing with contemporary reality. When was the last time someone (especially from the political arena) defined readiness for school in terms of inputs to the child? Such a definition might stipulate that children are ready for school when, for a period of several years, they have been exposed to consistent, stable adults who are emotionally invested in them; to a physical environment that is safe and predictable; to regular routines and rhythms of activity; to competent peers, and to materials that stimulate their exploration and enjoyment of the object world and from which they derive a sense of mastery. These factors alone would be better indices of readiness for school than any measureable aspect of child performance (e.g., Sameroff, Seifer, Barocas, Zax, & Greenspan, 1987).

Best Practices Models: "The Green Bible"

In recent years the dominant discourse of early schooling has been heavily influenced by the National Association for the Education of Young Children's publication *Developmentally Appropriate Practice in Early Childhood Programs Serving Children from Birth through Age 8* (Bredekamp, 1987). We will use the common shorthand DAP in our discussion.

DAP reflects a larger phenomenon that has emerged in education over the last 15 years or so—an emphasis on "best practices." Our use of the term "Green Bible" to describe the DAP reflects the religious fervor to which a certain practice or perspective is often adhered. As a result dialog is restricted rather than expanded. DAP is not the first, nor will it be the last example of this phenomenon. In the early 1980s, the School Effectiveness movement with its listing of characteristics of effective schools (see Purkey & Smith, 1983, 1985) was extremely influential. Then the search was for principals who exerted "leadership" because leadership was a factor differentiating effective from ineffective schools. When researchers eventually looked closely at the effect of principal leadership, they found, not surprisingly, that "leadership changes have different effects in different contexts and…these effects are slow to develop and of limited duration" (Rowan & Denk, 1984, p. 534).

Best Practice Discourse

Today one sees a large number of professional journals and monographs devoted to documenting "best practices." For example, the National Association of School Psychologists publishes volumes on best practices in school psychology (e.g., Thomas & Grimes, 1995). Recent edited texts also include a large number of chapters presenting evidence of what "works" with high-risk students (e.g., Waxman, de Felix, Anderson, & Baptiste, 1992).

This movement should be applauded for getting educators talking about what practices are effective with children. The work conducted in support of these documents can be painstakingly difficult, often involving years of testing interventions under very difficult conditions (Waxman et al., 1992). As is reflected by the DAP phenomenon, however, the whole-cloth assimilation of "best practices" by the educational community, and the overreliance on one or another model to explain, assess, or intervene with high-risk children, threatens to once again move our attention away from the relationship between children and schooling by focusing us on "program" or "method" and restricting dialogue to what is appropriate and inappropriate with respect to program and method.

The problem with "best practices" is not in the practices themselves, but with their designation as "best" or, in the case of DAP, "appropriate," along with the implicit and explicit designation of other practices as "worst" or "inappropriate." No practice can be the best or most appropriate in a world that is as complicated as the one in which high-risk children and schooling come together. Best practices defy contemporary reality. No practice, no matter how effective it might be in one context, will be as effective in another. Nor should those second-generation users of such practices spend time trying to do a better job of applying such practices with greater fidelity. Rigid insertion of methods or programs from one context into another cannot free systems to be more flexible and responsive to variety. It is imperative that educators counter the need for closure inherent in adopting a best-practices model. Such motivation toward closure is part and parcel of political discourse that wants effective schools and successful students, but has difficulty tolerating the uncertainty of experimentation.

Developmentally Appropriate Practice

DAP has been an important part of the ongoing contemporary discussion on early schooling, representing a serious effort to improve early schooling. Our criticisms are less of the book itself than of those for whom the Green Bible defines the discourse rather than being part of it. Early childhood educators pepper their discussions with the terms *developmental* and *developmentally appropriate*. To call a program or a classroom or a practice "developmental" or "developmentally appropriate" is to honor it with the ultimate stamp of approval. Thus the "stamp" gains in importance relative to the practices it suggests and ultimately limits discussion of alternatives.

DAP has been subjected to criticism by various scholars (e.g., Kessler & Swadener, 1992; Walsh, 1991). Our concerns here are with its limitations. We will discuss two. First, in assuming a consensus about child development that is more apparent than real, DAP presents a position that is at times Piagetian and, at others, as "vulgar-Piagetian" (described below). No mention is made in DAP of the major paradigm shift occurring in the study of child development, away from Piagetian structuralism toward a contextual systems perspective.

A second limitation of DAP or, more broadly, the discourse of developmentally appropriate practice, is that it presents little in the way of practically and theoretically grounded directions for working with children for whom school is a formidable challenge and who depend on school for all their formal learning. This shortcoming has unintended consequences in terms of DAP and its relationship to children whose risk of academic failure is high. For example, we see evidence in our study of a state-funded prekindergarten program that developmentally appropriate practice is seen as appropriate only for nonpoor, nonminority children (Walsh, Davidson, Ting, Enos, & Tsai, 1995). Teachers of "at-risk" preschoolers, influenced by their special-education colleagues, increasingly introduced behaviorist techniques into their classrooms. Given a strong tradition of behaviorist approaches for the children of the poor, our concerns are not without basis. As mentioned earlier, DISTAR, now most often found in special-education programs, was originally developed for the children of the poor, who, in the view of its authors (Bereiter & Engelmann, 1966) were not being well served by the more "developmental" approach of early Head Start. Our concern is that DAP may be contributing to the bifurcation of schooling experiences and methods of instruction along class and racial lines.

Piagetian Theory

Probably no other theoretical perspective has been as influential in the education of young children as Jean Piaget's. Piagetian theory is emphasized both implicitly and explicitly in DAP and we turn now briefly to this developmental perspective and its relation to discourse on risk.

The influence of Piaget's developmental theory has been pervasive. The vast majority of what educators, particularly early educators, know about child development is drawn from Piaget's theory of cognitive development. Piaget's theory is frequently referred to in pedagogy textbooks and in child development texts used in teacher training programs. Lawton and Hooper (1978) described the "extrapolation to the classroom of Piagetian theory" as "one of the more current preoccupations among certain developmental psychologists cum early childhood educators" (p. 169). Piaget himself did not develop a theory of instruction nor did he develop a program or curriculum.

Piagetian theory did not come to the fore in a theoretical or methodological vacuum. Instead it came into existing discourse on development heavily influenced by maturationist, behaviorist, and psychoanalytic theories. Although Piaget's theory represents a profound break from these perspectives on development, it was, to use his term, *assimilated* to fit into existing perspectives. As a result his theory has been misrepresented in unfortunate ways. Piaget's views on cognition and development are remarkably sophisticated in positing change as a function of dynamic, interactive forces operating in child and context. The concepts of assimilation, accommodation, equilibrium, and schema are essentially systems concepts. They describe action and reaction, dynamic interchanges of information and resources from which new structures emerge, which in turn influence subsequent interactions and structures. The process described is fluid and open.

But the context into which Piagetian theory was introduced and applied was one that viewed learning either as (1) an unfolding of potential that occurred largely as a function of time and biology, or (2) a function of contingencies in narrowly defined environmental parameters that acted to affect behavioral probabilities. The first view had no role for context; the second view, no role for anything other than context. So Piagetian theory, a theory that brought together context and child, was interpreted, and brought into practice, within dominant discourses that failed to recognize the nature of the relationship between context and child.

In discussions of paradigm shifts, there is a tendency to see an abrupt break with the past. Such clean breaks seldom occur. We do not suddenly begin looking at the world in completely new ways. The process of changing our basic understanding of something like learning and development can be painfully slow. Often, what appear to be paradigm shifts are more accurately described as "vocabulary shifts." This was clearly the case as regards Piagetian theory and early childhood education.

> Although the dominant theory of development in early education is Piagetian theory…practice is dominated by a form of vulgar-Piagetian theory. Vulgar-Piagetian theory uses Piagetian terminology and emphasizes the child's movement through invariant stages, but the mechanism for developmental change is not the equilibration or self-regulatory process, as Piaget argued (1970), but biological maturation. The child is seen not as actively involved in his or her development but waiting passively for nature to run its course. (Walsh, 1989, p. 387)

This vulgar-Piagetian perspective severely limits the capacity of educators to understand and influence the relationship between children and families and early schooling.

Piagetian theory itself, properly understood, has come to be viewed as having serious limitations. A number of contemporary developmentalists, for example, Bruner and Haste (1987), Donaldson (1978), Gelman (1979), Gelman and Baillargeon (1983), and Inagaki (1992), have rejected broad invariant stages and have critiqued Piagetian theory for seriously underestimating the cognitive and other capacities of children and for seriously neglecting the role of the cultural and the social in children's development. Rogoff's work (1990) very clearly indicates that notions of generalized stages tied to abstract reasoning tasks are poor indices of children's cognitive performance in real-world contexts and in structured settings. Resnick (1995) and Rogoff (1990) emphasize the situatedness of cognition and how social, cultural, and historical factors influence children's performance. For these "post-Piagetians" (Inagaki, 1992), Piaget's theory is viewed as inadequate for its over-reliance on fixed, abstract stages, and the absence of dynamic fluid properties.

SUMMARY

The discourse on risk and schooling can exert unintended but pernicious effects on advancing theory and practice by limiting the way we view risk and schooling. Whether the rhetoric of politicians, the debate about readiness, the search for best practices, or appeals to Piagetian truths, each discourse masks realities. Nonetheless the appeal of these discourses remains high. We turn now to specific models of school failure.

3

The Invidious Triangle

Two theoretical and political perspectives have dominated explanations for why children marginalized by ethnicity and poverty do not do well in school: the Cultural Deficit Model and the Cultural Difference Model. The deficit model places the blame on the home or home culture; the difference model blames the school. These locations comprise two corners of the invidious triangle.

The third location and corner of the triangle is the child. The practice of locating the source of failure in the child is as old as the psychometric movement and has been at the heart of the growth of special education. Locating failure in the child (by group) is essentially a genetic explanation. Although individuals have argued that some groups are not as intelligent as other groups, as members of ethnic groups were once considered below average in intelligence, we find such group-genetic explanations particularly troubling and not worthy of discussion. We also omit in our discussion Marxian and neo-Marxian structural explanations, for example, Bowles and Gintis (1976), Bourdieu and Passeron (1977), and Apple and Weis (1983). This work has failed to live up to its initial promise, and to the extent that it is empirical, it does not address the beginning years of schooling.

DEFICIT

The cultural deficit or, as it has also been called, the Cultural Disadvantage Model posits that children from poor or minority families struggle in school because they have been disadvantaged or deprived by their impoverished home and cultural backgrounds. Valencia (1986) describes it thus:

> Also known in the literature as the "social pathology" model or the "cultural deprivation" model, the deficit approach explains disproportionate academic problems among low status students as largely being due to pathologies or deficits in their sociocultural background (e.g., cognitive and linguistic deficiencies, low self-esteem, poor motivation). (p. 3)

The Cultural Disadvantage Model was very influential in the early years of compensatory early schooling. Connell noted, "In the 1960s and 1970s, the cultural deficit concept became folklore among teachers as well as policy makers" (1994, p. 131). Head Start was founded to ameliorate the disadvantage that poor and minority children brought with them from home to school. Sargent Shriver, OEO (Office of Economic Opportunity) Director, who was the driving force behind Head Start, described schools as being "as intimidating to these disadvantaged children as the inside of a bank to a pauper" (Zigler & Meunchow, 1992, p. 6).

A strength of the Model was that the implications for practice were clear cut: Make available to children in school that which they had been deprived of at home; and improve the situation at home, which Head Start attempted to do through parent involvement and providing health care services. But as an explanatory model, it remained inherently weak. It was unfair to the children and their families, and it took a very inaccurate and invidious view of nondominant groups and their cultures. Nevertheless, even though the words disadvantaged and deprived may no longer be used publicly, as an explanatory model, they remain alive and well in contemporary school hallways and elsewhere.

When anthropologists and members of nondominant groups objected to their cultures being described as disadvantaging their children in school and to their children being described as deprived, the reaction was simply to move away from this model and instead talk of cultural differences. It is important to note, however, that the two models differ significantly in where they place the blame for the child's failure. The disadvantage model places it in the child's home and home culture. The difference model places it in the school to which the child comes.

DIFFERENCE

With the introduction of the Cultural Difference Model children were no longer seen as coming to school "broken," but as different. In this model children come to school from nondominant cultures that are different from the dominant culture of the school. Because of the differences, miscommunication and misunderstandings are common. Children do not do well in school and are often perceived as being less capable than their peers from the dominant culture for whom school is a very familiar place. The implications of this model are also straightforward: Make the schools more culturally responsive to the children.

The Cultural Difference Model, although more palatable and respectful of nondominant cultures, has become increasingly problematic. Like the Contextual Systems Model, it focuses on the relationship between the school, assumed to be part of the dominant culture, and the home, assumed to be situated in a nondominant culture. Unlike our model, in the Cultural Difference Model the connection between home and school is the child, who moves from the familiar culture of home where her competence is evident to the unfamiliar culture of the school where she is no longer competent. The Cultural Difference Model has remarkable appeal and is the basis for a great deal of discussion taking place on the education of poor and especially minority children. Authors who advance the notion that African-American children perceive, understand, learn, or behave differently than European-American children, and that these differences are directly attributable to differences in culture (and not other influences on development) are arguing from a cultural-difference perspective (e.g., Heath, 1983; Shade, 1982).

Although an improvement over "blame-the-victim" models like the Cultural-Deficit Model, the Cultural Difference Model is limited. It must be specified, expanded, and unpacked in order to be useful. First, the Cultural Differences Model assumes an outdated and rather simple and static conception of culture, where culture is seen as a system of rules and structures that, although often hidden to the outsider, is to the insider both well known and constant. The definition of culture that emerged from studies of small, apparently homogeneous and isolated peoples, even if useful in those circumstances, is not applicable to the diverse, rapidly changing and overlapping cultures that make up the contemporary United States. Culture instead is much more dynamic, "a matter less of artifacts and of propositions, rules, schematic programs, or beliefs, than of associative chains and images that tell what can reasonably be linked up with what...collective stories that suggest the nature of coherence, probability, and sense" (Rosaldo, 1984, p. 140). One challenge to the Cultural Differences Model is that for many African-American children, and other children from the nondominant culture, differences within the nondominant group on dimensions considered critical to school success are as great as they are between the nondominant and dominant cultures. It is, in fact, an anthropological truism that groups vary as much or more within than between.

Second, the child is presented as alienated in an unfamiliar school, but no link is made between skills or lack of skills in school and the use of those skills in the home culture. A picture of discontinuity is presented, but the data supporting discontinuity are sketchy, and the explanation for discontinuity is often simplistic. For example, the educational community has been very taken with Heath's (1983) argument that certain linguistic styles, for example, the use of questions, vary dramatically between school and home for poor black children, and thus communication problems arise in school. This strikes us as a naive explanation that ignores the ability of human beings to communicate in remarkably difficult situations. It may well be that groups set up borders across which they agree not to communicate, but that is a very different matter from being unable to communicate. Also, in this picture of discontinuity, the very situatedness of learning and knowledge is ignored. Competence is not easily moved from one situation to the next. What one situation, in all its complexity, evokes from a child is very different from what another situation will evoke. If children are not communicating well in school, there is more going on than simple discontinuity of the type present in the Cultural Difference Model.

Third, as noted above, the cultural-differences explanation ignores the variation within any culture. Ogbu's (1981) often-quoted notion that all cultures raise their children to be functioning adults in that culture, masks the reality that in every culture some children become dysfunctional adults. In even the most homogeneous societies individuals find their way into prisons and other institutions. Marginality and dysfunction are parts of all cultures. And as cultures become pressured and rapidly altered by internal and external factors, it appears that the number of children who do not become functioning adults is increasing. What happens when cultures are raising their children to be functioning adults in a culture that will no longer exist when the children get to adulthood or will exist in a radically different form?

Thus, to assume that "failures" of nondominant-culture children can be attributed to cultural differences masks the fact that dominant cultures produce their own versions of "failures" with striking regularity. One problem with the focus on the underachievement of poor and minority students is that it draws our attention away from the reality of school failure that cuts across social class and ethnic lines. Even though the vast majority of children with whom we are concerned in this book come from nondominant cultures and/or poor families, it is also the case that not all WASPS do well in school.

Fourth, the model pays insufficient attention to powerful influences that cut across cultures, most notably, economic factors. Ogbu (1974) has shown persuasively that the Cultural Differences Model ignores the meaning that school has for the members of different subcultures given the economic opportunities available to them and the perceived link between those opportunities and school performance. Ogbu argues that if a culture perceives success in school as not being helpful economically, adults will not encourage their children not to do well and may in fact discourage them from doing well lest they be set up for later frustration when they discover that whatever their academic achievements their social mobility is limited by other structural factors.

Fifth, the Cultural Differences Model identifies only one type of risk: the risk that is created by the school's inability to bridge the gap between the culture at school and the child's home culture. Clearly this disjunction can create risk. Furthermore, evidence that risk due to cultural differences can be reduced by changing school curriculum and practice has been shown by the work of the Kamehameha Early Education Program (KEEP) (e.g., Au, 1979, 1980; Au & Jordan, 1981; Tharp & Gallimore, 1988). This private school for ethnic Hawaiian children was established in 1971 in response to the low achievement levels of poor Hawaiian children in the public schools. It is not clear to what extent this work with a single ethnic group, Hawaiians, can be generalized to multiethnic realities that many schools face.

Still, to the extent that this disjunction or discontinuity between school and home can contribute to a child's risk coefficient, it is but one of very many factors. Risk factors other than cultural differences are very real in the lives of children from dominant and nondominant groups, and these risks very much affect the development of children and their chances at succeeding in school. To be part of a population that is disproportionately poor, to be, for example, a rural Appalachian white, an African-American, a Mexican-American, not only increases the likelihood that one will face extended poverty, but also that one will face numerous daily life hazards related to poverty. For example, an Appalachian child faces a much higher-than-average risk of not having received prenatal care, having a low birth weight, not receiving adequate inoculations, living in substandard housing, attending a substandard school, being a victim of violence, and so on.

These are real risk factors with very real consequences for schooling. They are not simply matters of cultural difference. Furthermore, children of the dominant culture also become marginalized and face increasing risk due to many of these same experiences. Living in substandard housing or with unstable parents, or being exposed to domestic violence or maltreatment has negative effects regardless of culture. As persuasive as the Cultural Differences Model has been, with rare exceptions, for example, KEEP noted above, the educational programs or reforms that have been based on the Model have not had the intended and promised effects.

In summary, the Cultural Differences Model, like other models that emphasize and acknowledge the influence of culture on development and behavior (e.g., Bronfenbrenner, 1979; Bruner, 1990b; Rogoff, 1990), extends the discourse on risk by making educators aware of the importance of culture in children's learning and development in early schooling. But for the very reason that it attends only to the single dimension of culture, and a simplistic version of culture at that, the Cultural Differences Model does not begin to be comprehensive enough to address the range of conditions responsible for the terrible state of the relationship between children, families, and early schooling in this country.

WHERE IS RISK? THE INVIDIOUS TRIANGLE

As noted earlier, we have both spent much of our adult lives in schools—as teachers, researchers, and parents. Much of what we have heard in schools revolves around the identification, location, and solution of problems that children are having in school, or, as is perhaps more often the case, that adults are having with children. Many problems appear to be chronic and quite predictable, particularly if one ignores within-group variation—novice teachers have problems with classroom management and transitions (although some do quite well), poor children have problems dealing with classroom structure (although many get along wonderfully), and so on.

The source of the problems that children are having in school is most likely to be located by educators in one (or more) of three places:

the child, the family (i.e., home, home culture), or the school. These are not useful places to locate problems. A discourse that contributes to locating problems in one (or even two or three) of these places, in the absence of an emphasis on the interactions, transactions, and relationships among these places, will not advance an understanding of those problems.

When we locate a problem, we are not just "putting" it somewhere, we are also defining it, constructing it, and giving it a genealogy. If we locate a problem in the child, it becomes a different problem from the same problem located in the school, a problem of learning versus a problem with teaching. In fact, the move from a Cultural Deficit to a Cultural Difference Model was really about where to locate the problem of school failure. In the process, the very problem became different, as did, naturally, the proposed solutions. Locating risk in one of the three sites mentioned is "single-location discourse." The three strands of single-location discourse on risk result in the "invidious triangle" of child, home, or school pathology, with each discourse's attributions about failure and success resting on one of the points of this triangle. This triangle does not provide a strong base for schooling high-risk children. The child is falling somewhere through the middle.

It's in the Child

A long and strong tradition locates the problems that children have in school in the children themselves. The psychometric movement began and has thrived by showing that school success, and failure, was quite predictable based on a child's intelligence, assumed to be a rather fixed and quite measurable commodity (for an insightful and critical history of the psychometric movement, see Gould, 1981). If a child does not do well in school, it is because he or she simply lacks sufficient intelligence to do well. Over the years great progress has been made locating problems in children. No longer is the child limited only by intelligence, she or he may also be limited by, to name a few, dyslexia, an attention-deficit disorder, a learning disability, a processing disorder, a developmental delay, a behavioral disability, or an emotional disability.

Interestingly, one of the prominent differences between schooling in the United States and other comparable societies is in the attribution of success and failure (Stevenson & Lee, 1990). In comparing children schooled in several locations across the United States with those schooled in China and Japan, children, parents, *and teachers* in the United States overwhelmingly attribute school success and failure to innate, individual traits such as ability or intelligence. In contrast, children, parents, and teachers in the comparison countries attribute success and failure in learning to the effort of the child and skill of the teacher in arranging the instructional environment for learning. Thus in the United States, responsibility for success and failure in school is located in a much different place than it is in other countries, and the consequences of this location for how low achievement is addressed are apparent. The attributional differences among these countries is both a source of the problem and a consequence of years of frustration attempting to address the problem of high-risk children.

Locating problems in children is very popular—it is done often and is viewed as acceptable. It gets everyone, often even the child, off the hook of responsibility for the problem. Special education, as a field, reflects this assumption, and has contributed to its public acceptance. Despite evidence (empirical and otherwise) showing that boundaries between child performance and school context are quite blurry (Resnick, in press), educators and psychologists are quite content to find the reason for a child's difficulty with reading, or maintaining attention, in some hidden niche in the child's brain (Pennington & Ozonoff, 1991; Riccio, Hynd, Cohen, & Gonzalez, 1993), or in some profile of scores on tests of relatively esoteric abilities.

Several investigators point to advances in neural imaging, molecular genetics, behavior genetics, and mapping of the human genome as support for locating the cause of problem outcomes in the child's genes or brain. These arguments fail to acknowledge first and foremost, however, that nearly *all* studies of the neurology and biology of children with problem outcomes are fundamentally flawed with respect to identifying causal agents. These studies are typically cross-sectional in design, that is, they select children with a known problem (a learning disability, Attention Deficit Hyperactivity Disorder, etc.), examine neural or biological factors, and compare these values with those of children without such difficulties.

This design only tells us correlational patterns and nothing about causes. It tells us that *some* children who already have problems have different neural structures, biochemistry, or funny test-score patterns. Furthermore, these studies often fail to acknowledge that the very neural structures and biochemical values studied are themselves influenced by experience. Recent studies of developmental neurobiology clearly indicate that several of the neurological processes implicated in later problem outcomes are highly influenced by experience early in life (Cicchetti & Tucker, 1994; Greenough & Black, 1991). To argue that differences in test-score patterns or neurological findings from cross-sectional studies of already identified children somehow can be used to infer causality is misrepresentation. But these findings "fit" very well with dominant cultural explanations of school failure and result in the ready labeling and medication of millions of children who are having difficulty in school.

Ironically, "in-the-child" arguments do nothing to advance our efforts to educate children who may (most do not) have such biologically or individually based problems. What is an educator to do with a child whose genes, for the sake of argument, program her to not pay attention or to have difficulty decoding written symbols, or whose underlying neural structures and biochemistry are correlated with difficulties processing certain types of information? Like other simple explanatory systems for educational failures, the "in-the-child" approach ultimately truncates dialogue.

Even if compelling empirical evidence for locating educational problems within the child existed, *and it does not*, given our understanding of the intricate interdependencies of daily human life, one would expect from *educators* a reluctance to locate problems there. Remember the attributions of educators in China and Japan. Identifying disabilities as existing within a child, and not somewhere in the relationship between child and context, flies in the face of the highly varied outcomes reported for children who do have serious genetically based problems of one form or another. Consider the changes in expectations for Down's syndrome children seen over the past decades, and consider the developmental realities of a contemporary child with Down's syndrome compared to those of a "mongoloid idiot" of not long ago. The classic Sameroff and Chandler (1975) study clearly demonstrated that the wide range of individual differences in cognitive development in premature and low-birth-weight children were *not* a function of child characteristics but of context. But apparently, the human, or young human head, remains an attractive place for locating either problems or their sources. The illusion, of course, is that by locating a problem we are addressing it, when in fact by locating the problem we may well be justifying our failure to address it.

It's in the Home

Although the Cultural Deficit Model, in its explicit form, is no longer offered as a public explanation for school failure, it thrives sub rosa. In private conversation, in the hallways and lounges of schools and elsewhere, one hears explanations that attribute failure to the inadequacy of the home (or home culture). What, one is asked, can one expect of these children given the home life or lack thereof from which they come? In our own research (e.g., Walsh, Baturka, & Smith, 1992) we often heard cryptic explanations for why lowered expectations needed to be held for some children: "He's from the trailer park" or "from the subsidized apartments."

Both of us have spent considerable time in the homes of high-risk children and in reviewing the literature relating home factors to their success in school (e.g., Pianta, 1990). Without doubt the home environments of children contribute very heavily to their success or failure in school, as will be discussed in subsequent chapters. But just as an emphasis on ability and intelligence slant and distort approaches to educating children, so does a view that attributes all the blame for educational failure to homes. Again, as emphasized earlier, the "problem" is distributed across a wide range of factors, including homes, and also including the mental set that locates problems in one corner of the triangle.

It has been suggested that the term "at risk" is simply a way to resurrect the Cultural Deficit Model in more acceptable language (e.g., Cuban, 1989; Erickson, 1992). Richardson-Koehler (1988) commented, "[At-risk] has also take over from such descriptors as disadvantaged, low SES, underachieving, problem children; terms that describe populations of students for whom schools traditionally have been less than successful" (p. 1). A return to the Cultural Deficit Model, in locating the failure in the child and the home, places the problem outside the agency of the school. Educators cannot fix misfiring neurons or faulty genes, nor can they fix dysfunctional households. And they should not, it follows, be blamed for failing to do so.

It's in the School

The third corner of the invidious triangle originates, not surprisingly, from critics of schools. This corner of the triangle borrows from the Cultural Difference Model as well as, curiously, from conservative rhetoric on schooling and school choice. The Cultural Difference Model posits a discontinuity between the culture of the school and the home or home culture and sees the schools as failing to recognize or adjust for that discontinuity. The solution, for the Cultural Difference Model, is that schooling must be tailored to the cultural variability reflected in the classroom.

In contrast to the Cultural Difference Model as an early "liberal" criticism of schooling, the conservative views suggest that schools are no more than an embodiment of socialism, the welfare state, or secular humanism. Protected from competition, buffered by continual subsidies, schools become an entitlement program that eats budgets and returns little on the investment. The solution to educational problems, then, is to unleash market forces on the schools, promote school choice and competition, reward good teachers and punish bad ones, and remove as much regulation as possible from the enterprise of schooling (e.g., Chubb & Moe, 1990).

Critics (see Asher, 1994, for a review) have described the inadequacies of the conservative, market-driven approach to school reform, which is based on the very dubious notion that there exists in the world all these empty, good schools waiting for students. The approach is very likely to leave poor, minority children in the cold, without choice, and may very likely backfire against white middle-class students as suburban, high-quality schools become over-enrolled and are unable to rapidly expand and contract in response to the market, unless, of course, one envisions a world where schools rise up as rapidly as strip malls and then go bankrupt with equal rapidity.

Of course neither position advancing the notion that educational problems reside "in the school" provides a comprehensive explanation for what is perceived as the ever-rising rate of failed education in the United States. Locating the problem in the school has been remarkably popular in the last decade or more. Beginning with "A Nation at Risk," a myriad of reports have criticized the shortcomings of schools. Blaming schools is simply another example of locating the problem somewhere else and in the process removing responsibility from constituencies who have responsibility for the success of public education. Clearly schools need to change if the "bottom third" is to be well served by them, but the problem is a societal one, that is, a systemic problem not a school problem. It is a shared one, that can only be located *between* not *within*.

SINGLE-FACTOR EXPLANATIONS

The three corners of the invidious triangle each reflect a common approach to understanding schooling and its relation to the child/family system—the single-factor explanation. In the single-factor explanation, schooling is usually understood in terms of a single variable or construct of interest. Performance is reduced to achievement test scores; teaching is reduced to some facet of direct instruction, or a child's learning is reduced to time on task. Reforms target these single variables with equally singular actions, for example, longer school days, or a particular instructional strategy. At the child/family end of the equation, considerable attention is paid to factors such as "parenting styles," "parent-child interaction patterns" or "family intactness" that are thought to influence school success, independent of other influences (e.g., Ogbu, 1982). Each of these single factors encompasses a literature of its own, often generating a set of best practices and reform efforts.

Many of the factors identified as affecting school success have been derived from studies in which correlations between "single factors" are reported. These studies relate different factors within the Model to one another (mothers' social support and child's classroom behavior; teacher expectations and child achievement). Our criticism of these studies is not that in and of themselves they are inaccurate or invalid. Our concern is with the scope of the interpretation. It is a mistake to conclude that achievement is a function (only) of expectations, or to expect that raising expectations will raise achievement, as much as it is a mistake to think that improving mothers' social support will necessarily affect their children's school adjustment. The problem with single-factor studies is that they are evaluated in isolation instead of within a framework that both accommodates multiple factors (e.g., multivariate models or studies) and accounts for the multiple ways in which they interconnect (e.g., systems).

The assumption underlying efforts to improve schooling, or to improve the relationship between child/family and schooling systems by altering a single factor, is that there is a direct, causal relation between the single factor of interest and student outcomes. This is a fundamental problem in the interpretation (and at times the design) of many studies in education. For example, in the case of correlation between length of the school day (or year) and student performance, the assumption is that increasing school day by "x" amount will predictably and lawfully produce an increase in student performance of $F(x)$.

The linear-causal assumption is usually not articulated a priori by reformers and is masked in most research studies. This occurs in part because there is no alternative conceptual frame that can integrate multiple factors and influences. Correlations between length of school day and student performance and between family intactness and school performance could both be a function of neighborhood, school, cultural factors, or even curriculum or program effects. How can we understand how all these data fit together, and the activity of these factors in relation to one another?

Interestingly, the intervention literature tells us that change in a given outcome of interest (i.e., dropout rates, test performance) is a function of intervening into many of the factors identified in research: families, schools, and curriculum (Ramey & Campbell, 1991). Reforms that are comprehensively targeted at multiple factors produce the most significant change in outcomes (Holtzman, 1992; Schorr et al., 1991; Waxman et al., 1992). Our thesis is that complexity should not be an excuse not to reform schooling, but rather a cue to apply and develop alternative conceptual frameworks that can give rise to reform actions that recognize contemporary reality.

No model can account for all possible factors or relationships, but a useful model will allow one to show where and how a specific factor or relationship would fit. Plainly, single-factor linear models are inadequate for understanding the multiple relations across these systems. Although multivariate linear models add on factors, the resulting models are often clumsy and their notion of how to model the activity or interactions among the factors remains in terms of bivariate correlations. Arguing that school success is due to "this and this and this and this" is not much of an improvement over saying success is due to "this."

The single-factor approach to analyzing early schooling is highly reductionistic. Whether maturationist or behavioral in view, whether focused on effective schools, teacher empowerment, or some other aspect of schooling, this discourse on schooling and risk focuses on a "problem" and seeks solutions to that problem through manipulation of variables at that level. This approach does not recognize that the "problem" only has meaning within a larger whole and that efforts to address the problem must address the relation with the whole. The three corners of the invidious triangle used to explain risk (in the child, in the home, in the school) reflect the failure of current conceptual (and applied) models to consider broader units of analysis.

SUMMARY

All three explanations for locating risk fail to adequately account for the complexity of life's processes in relation to educating children. Of course schooling depends on children, homes/families, and schools. But schooling is not simply a function of one of these factors independent of the others, nor can one devise a simple arithmetic function to compute the proportion of schooling that accounts for each. The challenge of educating high-risk children is larger than these three elements, or their sum. For any given child, no one of these elements can be isolated from its co-action with the other two, and other elements, to explain school failure. Poor kids usually go to poor schools; rich kids usually go to good schools.

The politics of risk would have us identify children, or schools, or families as wholly responsible for the massive rate of failed schooling present in the United States. Each corner of the invidious triangle has its own constituency, and the forces attributing failure toward that particular corner are supported by that constituency. The point is not to remove politics from the discussion of risk but to identify and define the political elements in order to move discourse about the education of children beyond explanations that are, first, incomplete, and, second, proxies for political perspectives.

A conceptual model is required that locates the problem not in the child, the home, or the school, but in the relationships between child and family, and schooling, and the other individuals and institutions involved in schooling. Problems cannot be placed in some static location. Rather they are distributed across and among ever-changing contexts. They exist in constantly changing between-spaces. The relationships we seek to describe, understand, and ultimately work with are not just between school and family or between teacher and child, or child and parents, they are between dynamic patterns of interaction involving all these agents and actors.

The Contextual Systems Model provides a way of viewing children, all children, but particularly high-risk children. It provides a map for working with those children for whom school is a particular challenge. The CSM is a model of the interactions among children, families, schools, and the variety of contexts that affect these interactions over time. It attempts to model the complexity that is the reality of risk, and the reality of development. There is much to be learned from almost 30 years of concerted efforts to improve educational and life outcomes for these children. But a lot of what has been learned falls into the category of "this is complicated," especially when the goal is to improve educational and life outcomes. Throwing up one's hands at the complexity of the task contributes to the problem.

Educators need a lens that enables them to handle complexity without either oversimplifying it (as is the case in politically driven views) or being overwhelmed by it (which is seen in the ever-increasing movement toward frenetic change). Many of the efforts to address issues of success and failure in the early school years have lacked an adequate conceptual framework, particularly a framework that allows for a greater integration of educational policy and practice with contemporary perspectives on child development. Where conceptual frameworks have existed, they have been static and have not changed as understandings of children's development have expanded.

In a world in which political realities control so much of what can be done or developed, policy and practice are determined often by expediency, convenience, and appearances. These are weak foundations on which to build children's lives. Something about schooling welcomes a hegemonic discourse, perhaps the desire for final answers to persistent problems, for one correct and timeless way to educate children. Orthodoxy provides a comfort that ongoing conversation and debate does not. Where battles do rage in contemporary schooling, they are inevitably between competing orthodoxies. Missing is any sense of the importance of exchange of ideas and the construction of practice from the exchange. We would like to exchange some ideas.

Case Study: *Glenda*

Glenda is a seven-year-old girl living with her four-year-old sister, mother, and father in a community just outside the suburban ring of a major metropolitan area. Glenda is healthy, her parents have been reportedly happily married throughout her life, and her development in the areas of language, cognitive skills, and motor ability has been unremarkable. Glenda's mother works full time in a large company in the metropolitan area nearby, roughly a 50-minute commute. Glenda's father is a professional working 30 minutes away in another community. Both parents have worked full time throughout Glenda's life. Both are college educated with advanced degrees or training, both are professionals, and the family income approaches $100,000 per year.

Glenda has spent more than five years in full-time (or more) day care. Having a fall birthday, she was one of the younger children in her kindergarten class. Her mother dropped her off at the sitter's at 6:30 every morning, and she took the bus to the sitter's every evening until she was picked up by mother or father around 6:00 p.m. Her younger sister spent approximately 12 hours per day at the sitter's.

Observations of Glenda prior to her entry to kindergarten indicated she was a somewhat timid and reticent child who took few risks and was somewhat prone to portraying herself as fragile, although these characteristics were not extreme or debilitating in any way. She liked being with family and peers, and although somewhat controlling of her parents, she nevertheless sought them as sources of comfort and contact.

A day in the life of Glenda during kindergarten consists of the 6:30 a.m. drop-off, getting on the bus at 7:45, a full day of kindergarten, back to the sitter's until 6:00 p.m., dinner by 7:00, and bedtime around 8:00. Her parents view themselves as good, loving, actively involved parents; they arrange family activities on the weekends, read to their children, and are very involved in school. They take family vacations regularly at a beach house owned by a friend. Glenda attends a school within her community, approximately 15 minutes away from her home (and the sitter's).

Like many communities of this type, Glenda's town is under considerable growth pressure—there are 35 children in her kindergarten class with a part-time aide and parent volunteers. The community views itself as an upper-middle class bedroom community of families who do not want an urban or typically suburban lifestyle; the modal income and educational level in the community is consistent with this. School achievement is highly valued, and the school system is proud of having above-average test scores and high admission rates to college and university.

Glenda's kindergarten year is uneventful, although her teacher reports her to be somewhat immature and not as socially resilient as the other children. Reading instruction is a formal part of each school day, with instruction taking place in small ability groups. Glenda is reported to not be learning to read as fast as the other children in her group (she is in the "high" group based on her proficient expressive language skills)— she has difficulty mastering sound-letter correspondences, writing words and phrases, and decoding simple consonant-vowel-consonant sequences.

In the summer between kindergarten and first grade, Glenda's father is diagnosed with a life-threatening illness and begins treatment. Glenda's mother continues to work; and her father's disability insurance provides income as well. Glenda's father's illness is successfully treated, and he returns to work immediately following treatment. The parents acknowledge this has been a stressful time for the family, but do not talk in any detail about the impact of the illness or the experience. Despite possibilities of the illness returning, the family places this experience behind them.

In first grade, Glenda is placed in a class with 32 children and a teacher with five years of experience. Glenda continues to start her day at day care at 6:30, spends a full day at school, returns to the sitter's, and is picked up by her father at 6:00 p.m. on his way home from work. To observers Glenda appears more anxious than the previous year, some-what distractible and preoccupied, more dependent around her moth-er and father. She draws tentatively, and her stories suggest worries about disasters and monsters. She is reluctant to engage in active inter-action with peers; and although she gets along very well with every-one in the classroom, Glenda reports her best friends are the kids in the day-care setting who are a year or two younger.

Glenda likes to lie down in the afternoon and take a nap, or curl up in the teacher's lap in the reading corner, but this happens very infre-quently because the teacher is so busy with the rest of the children. The teacher does not know about Glenda's father's illness. Glenda contin-ues to have some difficulty in the reading program, struggling along in the middle reading group; and the teacher notices that her handwriting is also not up to standard.

The teacher has recently taken a workshop on learning disabilities (LD) and wonders if Glenda might have one. She discusses this with Glenda's mother, who tells her than she had mild problems in school as a child and that she has heard that LD runs in families. Parents and teacher decide to refer Glenda for special-education assessment so the specialists can figure out how to help her achieve to her potential.

Algozzine, Christenson, and Ysseldyke (1988) report that there is more than a 75% chance that Glenda will be found eligible for special ser-vices, and most likely will be labeled Learning Disabled. Glenda will receive pull-out services from the resource teacher each day for 30 minutes. There is a high likelihood she will receive those services for three or more years (see Singer & Butler, 1987).

This case poses a number of questions related to the discussion of risk and schooling to this point. Where is risk located? Are Glenda's problems in school a function of her own characteristics, her family, or her school? Can her problems be reduced to a single explanation, or traced to a single source? What kind of conceptual model can help educators understand Glenda, understand the difficulties she faces in school, and help them respond to her needs?

part two
Systems

4

A New Lens
The Contextual Systems Model

In this chapter we present a theoretical framework that builds on but goes beyond the frameworks that have informed the intervention programs of the past three decades or more. The need for a theory to guide our efforts to address the needs of children deemed high risk is pressing. This theory must help us understand the many ways in which failure comes to be and also provide directions for addressing that failure. The theory must be broad-based enough to integrate diverse theoretical perspectives in order to integrate and synthesize existing research.

Without a theoretical base, research findings, no matter how dramatic, have little heuristic value. Efforts to improve schooling based on them will have short-lived success if any. The Effective Schools movement, mentioned in chapter 2, provides an excellent example of what happens when reform efforts have no base in theory. The Effective Schools literature was a highly supported attempt to improve schooling for what were then most often referred to as disadvantaged children. This research and the resultant practice focused on technology and methods at the expense of theory-grounded practice. It focused almost exclusively on "what works," without attention to why or how something worked or did not. Various factors were identified as being associated with schools in which children were performing at higher academic levels than would have been expected given the student population of the school. These factors were then identified, packaged into reforms, and implemented in new contexts.

Not surprisingly, many reforms did not work as well in new contexts as they had in contexts in which they were "discovered." Attempts to understand why reforms did or did not work had no theory (of why the reform should work) to which to turn, and consequently no basis from which to make systematic alterations in the reform or the theory. As promised results did not materialize, what was once dubbed a "movement" faded as quickly as it emerged. The staying power of this movement was directly and inversely related to its attention to theory, in our view. Stedman observed, "What is staggering about all of this is that a careful reading of the effective school literature shows that the five-or six-factor formula *cannot be substantiated.* The vast majority of the studies…actually provide little support for these factors" (1987, pp. 215–216).

Efforts to improve schooling, especially as cast in terms of the relationships between children, families, and schools, require a theory or conceptual base comprehensive enough to accommodate the range of factors that effect this relationship. Improving schools is not simply a matter of changing the curriculum or changing the principal or initiating workshops on school climate. Any factor identified as associated with an effective school is surely the product of a developmental process in which very many factors interact over time to produce outcomes such as effective leadership. Workshops or training may help, but it is simpleminded to think that they will be the sufficient cause of effective leadership within a school. The differences between "effective" and "noneffective" schools are less important than how these differences came to be. The same criticism applies to the contemporary best practices movement. Inserting a certain practice or training a skill without concern for the context in which practices and skills develop, and how they develop, flies in the face of what is known about living, dynamic systems (Ford & Ford, 1987).

THE CONTEXTUAL SYSTEMS MODEL

Whatever the successes of attempts to address the educational needs of the children of the poor and minorities, the efforts have been hampered by political and other pressures and by the lack of a strong theoretical basis. Neither cultural models for explaining school failure nor the dominant theories of learning and development provide the necessary foundations for building educational programs for an increasingly diverse student population, one that faces life hazards that are intensifying at an alarming rate.

The Contextual Systems Model provides a lens through which to view (1) children and families who must daily struggle with a disproportionate share of "life hazards," (2) their relationship to schooling, and (3) the demands schools face in providing instruction to them. The model draws heavily from Developmental Systems Theory (e.g., Ford & Lerner, 1992; Sameroff, 1983; 1989) and sees development as framed by culture and history.

The Model is sufficiently open to accommodate a wide variety of child-rearing and preschool experiences for children as well as the wide range of schooling contexts and factors affecting schooling present in American public schools. Recent research on schooling and in child development paints a picture of enormous complexity in relation to the wide range of factors affecting performance on social and academic "tasks" in the early school years. One of the failures of current and past discourse on risk and schooling has been the narrow focus taken—certainly culture by itself, for example, cannot account for the variation in performance within a given school or between schools. Learning and reinforcement patterns are also inadequate.

Many factors are relevant to early schooling. Once identified they need to be unpacked within a model that explains their activity and their influence on schooling, and that gives rise to implications for how to arrange educational experiences. These factors are located in the many interactions across child, school, classroom, family, and community. Interactions in turn are embedded within patterns of interactions that form contexts for development. Thus, the Model must be able to account for interactions among individuals, groups, institutions, and patterns of interactions. Children interact with teachers. Ability groups interact within and across classrooms. Schools interact with community organizations. Child-rearing patterns interact with school discipline practices.

The Contextual Systems Model, in effect, provides a road map with which to locate and name the factors related to how children do in school and shows the roads between these factors—the interactions and patterns of interactions that we seek to explain and ultimately shape in desired directions. Figure 4.1 provides the beginnings of such a map.

Figure 4.1 is essentially a map with which to view the developing relationship among child and family and schooling, and the processes/systems that influence this relationship. The bottom of the figure shows the simplest schematic of the relationship among child and family and school. On the left side of the schematic is the child/family

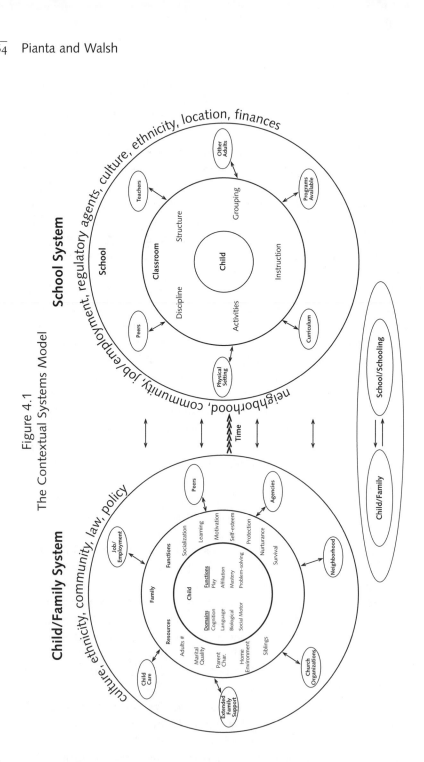

Figure 4.1
The Contextual Systems Model

system, which itself is composed of many subordinate systems. In expanded form these systems are represented above the simpler representation. To the right is the schooling system, represented in more complex form above with subordinate systems noted.

Encircling the child/family and schooling systems is a loop denoting the system that corresponds to the relationship between child/family and schooling. This relationship regulates the activities of the subordinate systems (child/family and school/schooling) with respect to one another and the goals of schooling. It is the key to understanding risk in the early grades. There are several features of this relationship that need to be explored here before addressing the more detailed, full-form model of this relationship.

The Contextual Systems Model recognizes that explanatory constructs and principles must be sufficiently flexible to accommodate the kind of contemporary realities educators face. In order to do so, the model makes the following assumptions:

- Any outcome is itself a multiply determined product of a large number of factors interacting over time.
- Mechanisms responsible for the development of this outcome are not reflected in linear relations between two or even three or four "causes."
- Multiple perspectives are possible and plausible in examining a given outcome, each yielding some degree of useful explanation.
- Complex realities of behavior and biology demand equally complex explanations.

We begin by defining and discussing terms. A *system* refers to an organized set of interrelated components each of which serves a function in relation to the activity of the whole system. A *living or open system* is one that exchanges information with the context in which it is embedded and that has self-regulating tendencies (Ford & Ford, 1987).

Systems are abstract units. They operate at many levels—societies are systems, families are systems, classrooms are systems, children are systems, brains are systems, certain behaviors are systems. Systems have subordinate and superordinate relations to one another, with units at a superordinate level having some degree of control or constraint over the activity of the subordinate units. A primary purpose of a system is to *regulate* the activity of its subordinate units with respect to a particular goal or function. Thus, a classroom system constrains the behavior of teachers and students with respect to the goals of the school; the brain, as a system, constrains the activity of the neurons and axons within it, with respect to organizing the behavior of the body.

A Relationship: Child/Family and Schooling

Educators seldom take seriously the idea that the child/family system and the schooling system are in relationship with one another. We attend to what one or the other is or is not doing, how they conflict at a given occasion, or how they may interact from time to time. The typical way of thinking about the connection between these two systems is reduced to "is the mother attending the PTO (Parent-Teacher Organization) meetings or school conferences?" "Does the child come to school dirty or late?" or "Has the teacher called the parent about the child's discipline or learning problem?" Thinking about child/family and schooling as systems, and thinking about their connection in terms of a relationship between systems, presents a new set of concepts and tools with which to address the challenges of educating children in high-risk circumstances.

First a word on *relationships*. Hinde (1987) and others (Sameroff & Emde, 1989) describe relationships as a particular form of a system, larger than the sum of the interactions between the subordinate units of which they are composed. Thus a marriage is "larger than" or superordinate to, what interactions take place between a husband and wife at dinner. The relationship between a parent and child is more than the sum of the parent's disciplinary actions and the child's compliance.

Relationships embody the characteristics of the subordinate units themselves—in the child/family side of our model factors like intelligence, family intactness, number of siblings are at work; and in the schooling side factors like teacher-child ratios, type of curriculum, and classroom rules are seen. These isolated features of subordinate units are embodied in interactions between the two systems involved in the relationship. In our Model this translates into interactions between teacher and child during reading instruction, or disciplinary interactions between child and principal, or interactions between the child and peers, or contacts between the child's parents and the teacher.

Hinde (1987) argues that relationships are more than just interactions. *Over time*, through repeated contact, memory, feedback and feedforward processes, interactions form fairly stable patterns, give rise to expectations, and begin to have a quality separate from the interactions themselves. An example of *feedback* processes would be the sense of self that one gets from others' perceptions of oneself. A *feedforward* process would be the sense of self that one brings to interactions with others.

In fact, evidence suggests that relationship-level factors (such as quality, type, etc.) begin to influence the interactive behavior of individuals in the relationship, such as when a teacher does not contact the parent of a discipline problem because she knows that "it won't do any good anyway" or when parents fail to attend meetings at the school in part due to feelings of embarrassment and lack of connection based on their previous schooling experiences.

A fundamental point regarding the Model, and its application to risk, is that relationship systems exist between the child-family and schooling systems *regardless* of their quality (good or bad), the nature of the contact between the units (positive vs. negative, engaged vs. disengaged), or the even lack of contact. It is not the case that no relationship exists.

All parents, even those without children in school, even if very alienated from schooling, have experiences with schooling and with their own children, that regulate (constrain, organize) their behavior toward their child in relation to schooling, and influence their children's behavior toward school. Schools approach new children and families not as blank slates, but with knowledge sometimes gained from systematic screening programs, or through stereotyping, or through expectations based on years of experience (about what "five-year-olds are like" or "what boys are like"), or through the available knowledge base.

Relationships can be rich, multilayered, interactive, and positive; they can be unidimensional, disengaged, and negative, or they can be anything in between. Nonetheless, they exist as relationships, and as systems composed of subordinate systems, and embedded within superordinate systems, whatever their form.

Why think about these entities as systems or in terms of their relationships with one another? In part because doing so makes possible a language that can accommodate some of the complexity involved. Many factors relate to school achievement. A model must be able to talk about those factors, and the dynamic interplay they have with one another. Also, the concept of relationships, as applied in general systems approaches, implicitly denotes a component of time. Relationships take time to develop. There are feedforward and feedback loops involving time (the effects of memory and expectations), and there are specific principles governing behavior in relationships and change in the nature of relationships that are directly useful to the problems we are facing—how to explain the breakdown in connections between child/family and school and how to identify and martial resources to improve these connections.

The extended model, depicted above the simple schematic (p. 64), describes in greater detail the systems and interactions (i.e., the "locations" and "roads") involved in the relationship between the child-family system and the schooling system. On the left side of the figure are factors and systems related to the child-school side of the relationship. On the right side are factors and systems related to schooling. Both sides of the Model are depicted as systems in their own right. The child-family system involves multiple influences, different levels, and a large number of relations among influences, all of which work together to regulate developmental outcomes for the child who enters into the relationship with schooling. Similarly, multiple influences, contexts, and subsystems work together to regulate schooling. The Model depicts the child-family and schooling systems as separate for the purposes of discussing and focusing on the relationship between the two systems, but one might argue that for the purposes of another analysis, both are subsystems within a larger system affecting the child's development.

Many of the systems depicted in the Model (e.g., family, school, peers) can be thought of as *contexts for development*. That is, each of these systems is a niche, or environment, which interacts with the child, or provides some form of input to the child. Graue and Walsh (1995) describe context thusly:

> A context does not merely contain the child and her actions; contexts are *relational*. They shape and are shaped by individuals, tools, resources, intentions, and ideas in a particular setting, within a particular time. Contexts are not static, to be captured by a series of descriptive variables in a regression equation (Gaskins, Miller & Corsaro, 1992). Instead, contexts are fluid and dynamic, constantly reconstituting themselves within activity. Contexts are inherently social, reflecting and framing interaction (Wertsch, 1985). The most important facet of any context is the other people who share a particular here and now. (p. 143)

Thus systems depicted in the model can be thought of in terms of social systems, social interactions, and constructed meanings that take place in a setting and over time.

In the Contextual Systems Model, the child is presented within the family, and both child and family are linked with a number of other contexts that influence their behavior and adaptation. These contexts include child care, job/employment, neighborhood/community stresses and resources, extended family and support networks, church and other organizations, peer groups available for the child and family members, and government/agencies. These contexts are in turn embedded within various cultural and subcultural contexts. All of these contexts can influence family and child development and in turn affect the relationship between the child-family and school.

As regards the child and family, the Model details a number of key elements that are relevant for schooling. At the family level these include marital status and quality; availability of adult resources; siblings; parent characteristics (e.g., intelligence, education, personality features, developmental history); and quality of the home environment (structure, availability of materials). These aspects of the family context serve a number of functions for the child including: socialization, learning, motivation, self-esteem, supervision/protection, communication, nurturing, and so on. None of these can be viewed as static, isolated factors even though that's the way they often appear when discussed in research articles. They are dynamic, interconnected, and interdependent.

At the level of the child, the model posits a number of domains of development as well as functions. Domains of development include cognition and associated learning processes (memory, attention); language; emotions; social behavior; biology (genes, physiology); and motor skills. Functions executed by these domains of development include play, problem solving, attachment, movement, communication, motivation, self-esteem, and interactive skills.

On the right side of Figure 4.1 (p. 64), the Model includes contexts and systems related to schooling. The large circle includes contexts and systems that exist within the school, and circles outside of that reflect influences external to the school. Within the boundaries of the school are included the influences of peers; teacher(s); other adults (principal, aides, coordinators); program availability (chapter 1, special education); materials (computers, books); the curriculum (what is supposed to be taught/learned); classroom-level influences such as rules and schedule; and school-level influences such as rules and schedule. The influence of these factors is mediated through discipline, instruction, structure, grouping, and other activities, such as recess and lunch time.

External to the school are a number of systems with influence. These include, to list but a few: the neighborhood and community in which the school itself is located (safe, dangerous, restrictive, open); employment conditions that affect the availability of adult roles and the mechanisms by which schools link children with those roles; and regulatory bodies, such as local governments, school boards, state agencies, and groups such as the PTO. Again, these contexts and systems are embedded within the larger system of subculture and culture, including ethnicity, race, region, urban, suburban, and so on. As was the case with the child/family system, relations among components within the schooling system are bidirectional and multidirectional, and they are organized and patterned. They tend to be reinforcing of one another, and ultimately, to create a network of relations that itself has its own properties over and above the properties of any individual relation or set of relations.

A crucial aspect of the Model is the focus on the quality of the relationship between the two major systems. This relationship is in part a product of the connections between the interactions of individual units within those major systems, or better, between patterns of interactions within different systems. We give an example later in this chapter of the relationship between child-peer interactions in the child-family system and child-peer interactions in the schooling system. The greater dissimilarity between these types of interactions in terms of expectations, behaviors, skills, and goals, the more likely the relationship between the child-family and schooling systems will be strained, and the more likely this situation will become a risk factor for the child. These cross-system relationships are depicted as bidirectional arrows connecting the child-family and schooling systems in Figure 4.1 (p. 64).

The final, and perhaps most important element of the model is *time* or *history*. The passage of time is depicted as an arrow running through the middle of the child-family and schooling systems. Time is critical to the model for several reasons. First, by including time as an "input" to a model of child-family and schooling relationships, the model is explicitly developmental. The inclusion of time also allows the Model to apply developmental principles to the analysis of this relationship, and to risk as it is present in this relationship. Second, time introduces a dynamic quality to the interactions and connections among elements of this Model. That is, we can now consider how feedback and feedforward processes operate with respect to these relations. In this sense, the Model pushes us past consideration of simple correlations between, for example, mother-child interactions and teacher-child interactions, or cultural influences on schooling, to a consideration of how these factors change in relation to one another.

To put it another way, the introduction of time makes it possible to examine how history affects present interactions, as well as how present conditions influence subsequent outcomes. Including time allows for the analysis of how the child's relationships with adults (based on interactions with parents and child care providers) influence their interactions in the classroom with teachers, and in turn, how these classroom interactions feed back on, and alter, interactions with parents and child-care providers. Including time forces a focus on how expectations of parents (based on their own experience and history) create perceptions, beliefs, and behaviors toward their child's schooling experience that alter and constrain that experience and in turn that are changed by that experience. These are critical processes for the understanding, identification, and ultimately the amelioration of risk because they point to processes and mechanisms that account for stability and change. Without an explicit role for time, any model is limited in its ability to explain process.

The Contextual Systems Model bears surface resemblance to Bronfenbrenner's (1986) recent formulation of the ecosystem model in which he adds a new system, the chronosystem. In the revised model, the chronosystem adds the effect of time, and changes in relations among systems that occur over time. In addition, it recognizes that history, or the passage of time, itself has an effect on subsequent development. Sameroff (1983, 1989) advances a model similar to Bronfenbrenner's in the emphasis on transactions between systems across time. In Sameroff's model, genotype and environment transact—or interact over time—to produce behavioral phenotypes. In turn, phenotype, genotype, and environment influence each other as time progresses. Like Bowlby (1969), Bronfenbrenner and Sameroff argue that time, or history, has an effect on subsequent development, and that current outcomes cannot be wholly explained even by perfect knowledge of present circumstances.

We emphasize the organizational aspect of the model and of systems in general. The multiple factors and contexts represented on the left and right sides of Figure 4.1 do not have independent, or even additive effects on development. Instead, these systems are interrelated, co-active, with effects that are bidirectional and multidirectional. Child factors influence family and school factors *and* vice-versa. Child factors influence multiple factors within the child-family system (such as siblings, peers, and child care). One can imagine double-headed arrows shooting among all aspects of the Figure. There are patterns of interactions (i.e., relationships) between systems, for example, people, institutions, and cultural groups. Thus we speak of the relationship between parent and child, between family and school, and between aspects of parent-child interaction and teacher-child interaction (e.g., sensitivity or lack thereof).

Furthermore, activity between and among systems is organized: patterns of activity are predictable and make sense based on previous activity. The multiple levels and systems within this larger child/family and schooling relationship "fit" together. The alienated parent's behavior toward a teacher who has labeled his or her child with an attention deficit disorder makes sense based on that parent's history and the child's developmental history. The failed attempts of predominantly white, middle-class schools to accommodate the wide range of individual differences of children makes sense based on school history, how teachers and administrators are trained, and so on.

From the Mountains to the City

We present below a brief example to illustrate the Model. Consider child-family system A and schooling system B. Loretta, whose family has recently immigrated from rural Appalachia to the city, lives in a trailer park with other immigrant and transient families—system A. She arrives in kindergarten in City School, System B. As in the Model, the school as a system is related to other systems. Thus even though it is part of the dominant cultural system, it also overlaps to some extent with system A—other Appalachian immigrants have attended the school over the decades. The city itself has absorbed aspects of Appalachian culture after years of assimilating immigrants. Nevertheless, Appalachian children, particularly recent immigrants, tend to be at the bottom of their classes.

At this point the Contextual Systems Model appears to be little different from a Cultural Differences Model. There are, however, important differences. The first is that our model specifies connections between interactions, not only between individuals or between individuals and institutions. Second, the Contextual Systems Model is built on a more developed conception of culture. Culture is seen not as a set of shared rules but as constantly changing transactional relations and understandings and is perhaps best thought of as a constantly changing and ambiguous shared text, which one must continually interpret. Third, we assume a wide range of variation in interactions within a given cultural system and a great deal of fluid overlap between cultural systems, where the Cultural Differences Model portrays a

world with little or no variation within cultures and little or no overlap between them. And finally, because our Model is a developmental
model, time or history is an explicit and critical factor.

Consider the interactions between Loretta and her peers in her
home culture A. These interactions may be seen within the norms of
system A as being mature or immature, as valued or not valued, as
gender appropriate or not, etc., and as anything in between. They may
be seen differently by different people, for example, by mother, father,
grandparent, and, of course, peers. These interactions may also be seen
as particularly important or defining to the cultural system, that is, as
a way of asserting membership in a given system, or they may be seen
as not particularly defining. For example, at any given historical
moment, certain ways of dressing, wearing one's hair, or speaking may
be seen as critically important to group identity, whereas at other
moments other practices or relationships may be seen as defining such
identity. We return to the notion of culture as a constantly changing
and ambiguous shared text.

Loretta then goes to school, a cultural system, which is located
within some version of system B, the dominant system, and overlaps
with other cultural systems. Here the Cultural Difference Model
ignores the extent to which school culture is itself a variation of the
dominant culture and the extent to which children, even from the
dominant culture, must inevitably be enculturated into the culture
of the school. Within the school culture, Loretta enters into peer
interactions, within the classroom, on the playground, in the lunch
room. Her thick mountain dialect may elicit one response in the
classroom and another very different one on the playground where
she find peers with similar accents.

We emphasize the differences between different aspects of school,
for example, the classroom and the playground. In order to adequately
study peer relations in schools, researchers must move out of the classroom and into the lunchrooms and playgrounds for the simple reason
that in many classrooms peer interaction is constrained. Further,
school is not a single entity. Children may do well in some aspects of it
and struggle with others. The child's interactions with peers in the
home culture A may be expected and valued and yet conflict with the
expected and valued relations with peers in school. This is, in fact,
common, and has been documented by many researchers, for example, D'Amato's (1988) study of ethnic Hawaiian children, in which he
showed that children's sense of peer solidarity conflicted with school
expectations of competition.

Most cultural difference explanations, to the extent that they compare how individuals function in two cultures, compare expected behavior with expected behavior and overgeneralize the extent of this behavior, that is, that all children from one cultural group exhibit a certain expected behavior with little or no within-group variation. Situations in which, for example, an interaction pattern in the home culture A that is not valued or expected, but which may or may not then match more closely an expected interaction in school culture B, is neither allowed nor explained. Nor is the within-culture variation that is the rule allowed. For example, a parent may approve of a child's peer-interaction patterns whereas a grandparent may not. Interaction patterns that are acceptable in one classroom or while one teacher is supervising recess may be totally unacceptable to another teacher.

The Contextual Systems Model in fully developed form depicts the distributed nature of risk and points readily to practice and research. It moves the discussion of risk away from the individual and into the larger cultural and historical systems within which the individual finds him or herself and within and between which children must make sense of their lives. It reflects contemporary reality.

SUMMARY

We have called attention to the relationship between child-family and schooling systems, and factors that influence this relationship over time. Implicitly we have advanced the idea that risk is *distributed* across the child-family and schooling systems, that it is not a characteristic of a child, or a family, or a school (the invidious triangle), but instead it is a *characteristic of a system,* specifically, the relationship between these two major systems, child-family and school.

In the Contextual Systems Model risk factors are located not within the child or the family or school but in the organization of these systems: in the patterns of interaction between the child, the family, and other individuals, institutions, and conversations within and across given cultural systems. Risk is distributed: everyone shares some piece of responsibility.

Time is posited as a critical variable in this relationship. Time is necessary for defining a relationship, and accounting for the influence of history and experience on present interactions between the two major systems. Loretta is not the first Appalachian immigrant to enter kindergarten at City School. She comes into an ongoing history of children arriving at school fresh from the mountains. Also, her relationships with school, teachers, and children changes across time.

5

General Systems Approaches to Understanding Early Schooling and Risk

Understanding schooling in the context of contemporary American society is a most challenging task. As society has become increasingly complex, so too has schooling. Witness the myriad reform efforts that have been applied in school contexts since the 1983 *Nation at Risk* report, and the subsequent evaluations of those efforts as mostly inadequate and sometimes misguided (Sarason, 1991). In 1992 Patricia Albjerg Graham, president of the Spencer Foundation, rued, "We were doing a lousy job 20 years ago, and we're not doing a better job now. Twenty years ago it didn't matter as much" (Editors of *Education Week*, 1993, p. xiv).

It is not uncommon to read reviews suggesting that efforts to improve some aspect of schooling (e.g., instruction) failed to meet expectations because some other aspect of schooling (e.g., school organization, principal effectiveness, teacher preparation) was not adequately addressed in the initial reform effort (e.g., Holtzman, 1992). Thus complexity is embraced as a reason why reforms fail, and after enough experience with failure, a reason why reform cannot and should not be attempted (Sarason, 1991). Complexity becomes a euphemism for passivity and giving up (Kozol, 1991).

The Contextual Systems Model embraces the complexity of early schooling. It does not attempt to reproduce the complexity of contemporary reality, but instead offers a framework that simplifies reality to the point that one can comprehend it without reducing that reality into something else entirely. Schooling in the early years is not reduced to whether the child knows certain facts, or how many children are in the classroom, or from what social class the child comes. It is seen in terms of systems, interactions, and relationships. The Model accounts for the web of interactions among child, school, classroom, family, and community: the systems that regulate a child's development. It accounts for interactions among subordinate systems nested within each of these systems, for example, between ability groups within classrooms, between children and step-parents within families, and between the individual school and the district administration.

The Model maps the systems we seek to understand and change. But just mapping these multiple systems is not enough. A coherent set of principles is needed to understand the activity of these systems, how they behave, how they change, and ultimately, how to predict their functioning with respect to the outcomes of schooling. In this chapter we present a series of principles derived from General Systems Theory (GST) (Ford & Lerner, 1992; Sameroff, 1989; von Bertalanffy, 1968) and apply them to the Contextual Systems Model. The discussion focuses on those principles that can be applied to understanding developmental processes, with an emphasis on how they can be applied to early schooling.

GENERAL SYSTEMS THEORY

GST has a long history in the understanding of biological, ecological, and other dynamic regulatory systems (Ford & Ford, 1987). Its concepts and principles allow for the description and analysis of systems—sets of interrelated parts that act in organized, interdependent ways as whole units. Emphasis is placed on understanding the behavior of the parts in relation to the unit as a whole, and in understanding the dynamic properties of the whole. GST concepts have recently been applied to child development by Ford and Lerner (1992) in what they call Developmental Systems Theory, and which bears many important similarities to Vygotsky's ideas.

The Contextual Systems Model applies GST to a broad array of systems involved in the education of young children. The GST concepts presented in this chapter are equally applicable to all the systems represented in the Contextual Systems Model. These principles provide a vocabulary with which to integrate analysis of the multiple factors that influence young children. As we discuss these principles of systems analysis we will draw on examples that reflect their application across many types of systems. We invite the reader to apply the concepts to systems present in the school contexts with which they are familiar. It should become very clear that terms such as "readiness to learn," "skill acquisition," "direct instruction," "effective schools," and even "at-risk children" are not consistent with this framework.

Co-action

Child/family and schooling are each complex and interdependent systems, at the same time subordinate to larger systems, and superordinate to lower-level systems that act in concert (for better or worse) with one another. The activity of these systems can be though of in terms of *co-action* (Gottlieb, 1991).

Co-action refers to the premise that activity of a given system, for example, the brain, or the classroom, is not independent; it relies on activity elsewhere, and itself affects the activity of other systems. Thus this web of systems acts together, in concert, and this co-action is organized. That is to say that the co-activity (the interdependent actions of multiple systems and multiple levels) is nonrandom. It is patterned and predictable (to some degree although never completely), and there are more or less sophisticated or complex ways in which organization is present (Greenspan, 1989; Sameroff, 1983).

Out of the co-action of the child/family and schooling systems, inside and out of school, the child constructs achievement or competence (Sameroff & Chandler, 1975). The co-action process is highly dynamic, active, and organized. It recognizes both history (what is past affects the present), and the future (goals exist within present status).

Types and Levels of Systems

A comprehensive discussion of the influences on children's learning and development acknowledges systems at several levels, as discussed by Bronfenbrenner (1979). Our discussion addresses systems that range from distal to proximal. The systems include culture, small social groups, dyads, the child, behavioral systems, and genetic/biological systems (see Figure 5.1).

Each of these systems is a context for development, and each carries with it a particular mechanism for influencing the behavior of other systems, or in other words, influencing child outcomes. Bronfenbrenner (1979) provides one of the more detailed explanations of differentiated contexts in terms of systems nested within each other, each with increasingly indirect influence on development as they move to broader levels.

Figure 5.1
Types and Levels of Systems

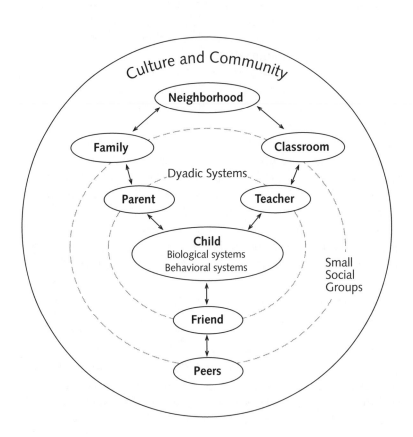

Sameroff (1989) describes the influence of contexts/systems using his concept of the *environtype*. Within this perspective, the environment (in this discussion, contexts) is conceptualized to have as powerful a regulatory influence on development (the child) as genetics. More importantly, Sameroff differentiates levels within the environtype that regulate development in specific ways. The influence of different contexts is embedded within codes that prescribe regulatory actions of the system vis-à-vis the child. These regulatory actions shape the proximal context in which the child must adapt.

Cultures and Large Communities

At the most distal level, cultures and large communities have an enormous impact on the education of young children. Although many readers may argue that we should split this level into several levels, we refer to systems typically known as cultures, subcultures, states, communities, etc., within this broad, global category of culture. Cultures and communities regulate the behavior of individuals and smaller social groups through creating, organizing, and maintaining roles within the larger group (Boulding, 1985).

Sameroff posits a set of cultural codes embedded within a culture's (or subculture's) *developmental agenda*. One way of thinking about a culture's developmental agenda is as the shared timetable for developmental milestones or generally held beliefs and expectations for child development. The developmental agenda is a series of culturally defined points in the child's life when the environment is restructured to provide different experiences to the child. These restructurings include toilet training, attending preschool, entering school, being taught to read, increased academic expectations, or testing programs linked to age or grade that sort children into different education tracks. These environmental restructurings are large-scale, long-term actions on the part of contextual forces—called *macroregulations* in Sameroff's model.

It is important to recall that many, if not all, enactments of cultural codes tend to be keyed to the chronological age of children in that population, not the developmental level of an individual child. In this way macroregulations may induce, or trigger, failure of one sort or another. Powerful contextual challenges to the child (maintaining peer relations, doing seat work) enacted based on chronological age (or some proxy) may exceed the child's capacity to adapt. They may require certain skills or capacities, or assume previous developmental successes that are not part of the child's life history or present status.

For example, when the typical high-risk child is placed in a classroom situation requiring familiarity with print, skills in using adults as helpful resources and symbols to mediate experience are required for success. Macroregulations of this sort increase the child's risk when they are beyond what Vygotskyan theory calls the zone of proximal development (ZPD) or when no ZPD is provided for the child. The ZPD refers to the range of competencies children can show, beyond what they typically demonstrate, when they are appropriately challenged and supported by a skilled teacher. Either too great a challenge for the developmental level of the child, or too little support to meet that challenge will result in some form of what is sometimes called "child failure" or "school failure," but what we call failure of the child/family and the school systems to communicate.

Families and Small Social Groups

At the next level, moving from the distal to more proximal, are systems of families and small social groups (peer groups, gangs, church groups, schools, classrooms). These groups are highly concerned with the regulation of the individual child's behavior and development, and a large part of their activity toward the child is oriented to the goal of producing individuals who adequately fulfill roles in the family and in smaller social groups seen as the larger social structure (culture).

At this level, codes within these social groups regulate the behavior of individuals with respect to the goals of the small group, which may or may not be consonant with the cultural developmental agenda. One purpose of families is to raise children to fulfill certain needs of the culture. One purpose of schools is to provide workers for the "global economy" and socialized individuals who can be productive members of society.

Regulatory actions based on family or classroom-level codes in Sameroff's view operate within a shorter time span than cultural code regulations and reflect the repeated demands of living together in small social groups and meeting the larger developmental agenda. Sameroff calls these *mini-regulations*. Care-giving practices such as feeding and discipline, expectations for performance, and patterns of emotional expression allowed within the group are all coded at this level and enacted through regulations that involve rules or the behavior of adults. These regulatory influences allow the group to function as a cohesive social unit. Family- and classroom-code influences on risk are apparent, for example, in family expectations for performance and discipline practices in school.

Dyadic systems (child-parent, peer-peer, parent-parent, teacher-child) play a major role in the development of children and the regulation of their behavior within small social groups. Over time, dyadic interactions conform to patterns and rules that constrain the behavior of the individuals. At this point the dyadic system is described as a *relationship* (Hinde, 1987) in which the behavior of the two subordinate units (individuals) take on properties of a whole.

Regulation is coded at this level and enacted through what Sameroff terms *individual codes.* With respect to relationships between adults and children, these codes involve the socializing agent's (caretaker, teacher) accumulated feelings and beliefs about their behaviors with children—what works and does not work—their motivation styles, and their goals of interaction with children in general and specific children in particular. These feelings and beliefs are enacted in very brief, often subtle aspects of moment-to-moment interaction with children (micro-regulations). The qualities of this interaction are described not by what is being done by the adult or child (i.e., feeding, punishing, attending) but by *how* it is being done in relation to the other. Thus constructs such as reciprocity, sensitivity, coordination, and synchrony are considered important (Sameroff, 1989).

Considerable evidence shows that the quality of patterns of dyadic interaction play an important role in adaptation of the child within the given context—home or classroom (e.g., Howes & Hamilton, 1992). Furthermore, many developmental problems can be linked to individual (adult or peer) codes that shape the child's proximal context (home or classroom) in ways that erode its function as a Zone of Proximal Development. This can happen because the code is inconsistent with previous developmental history (too challenging) or with codes present in other contexts. For example, a teachers' style of relating to children may assume certain prior experiences in relationships on the part of the child—a style that is aloof, business-like, and tends to remain emotionally distant from children may trigger different responses from children depending on whether the child had a history of emotionally close, warm, and available care from an adult.

The Child As a System

At the next level of analysis is the developing child as a system. At this level the focus is on the systemic properties governing the organization of behavior across many developmental systems (motor, cognitive, emotional) to produce an integrated whole (the "whole child") with properties of identity and stability. One is concerned at this level with the fact that motor, cognitive, social, and emotional development are not independent entities on parallel paths, but that they are integrated within an organized, dynamic process.

In this way, consideration of one aspect of the child (e.g., assessment of cognitive development or reading achievement) is an artificial endeavor. Testing and evaluation of children often falls into this trap of drawing somewhat artificial boundaries between these component systems. The whole child, as a system, however, cannot be explained in terms of its parts, much less in terms of one part. Taking a developmental systems perspective, many argue that assessment should focus on broad indices reflecting integrated functions across a number of behavioral domains (Greenspan & Greenspan, 1991). *Competence* is such an index, as is the term adaptation (Sroufe & Waters, 1977).

The primary point is that when considering the child as a developing system, we are not focusing solely on one aspect or domain of functioning, such as cognition, but on the organization of behavior from multiple domains with respect to particular situational or developmental demands. We discuss this perspective in much greater detail in the next chapter, but even with this cursory treatment it is easy to see that this conceptualization of the child and child functioning has many implications for schooling. Assumptions about performance, indicators of progress, and targets of instruction are all affected by viewing the child as a developing system.

Biological Systems

It is interesting, and troubling, that increasing attention is being paid to genetic/biological systems in explanations for risk and school failure. Genetic "causes" have been offered for such functional problems as reading failure, overactivity and attention problems, and conduct problems (Pennington & Ozonoff, 1991; Riccio et al., 1993). The research pointing to biological or genetic reasons for school failure is too often misinterpreted to suggest a "causal" role for biology and ignores the reality that biological systems are embedded in, and interact with, other systems (Gottlieb, 1991; Greenough & Black, 1991). At best, these studies must be viewed in light of evidence that biochemical and genetic activity are affected by experience and environmental parameters (Gottlieb, 1991), and that biological influences on behavior operate within the larger systems' influences as described previously. That this is the case is so obvious, one can only wonder at the ease with which biological interpretations are made for children's problems, reflecting, in part, the maturationist view of school readiness and achievement. These interpretations place responsibility for school progress on some unknown, unseen force within the child, blaming not so much the victim, that is, the child, as his or her gene pool. The central role of context is ignored.

Summary

Cultural, small social group, and individual adult codes (and their corresponding regulatory actions toward children) are organized together and frequently delivered as a package that has been referred to as a "developmental niche" (Super & Harkness, 1986). This niche reflects the organized patterning of these codes, itself an influence on children. In a stark example of a developmental niche, Garbarino and colleagues (Garbarino, Dubrow, Kostelny, & Pardo, 1992) have written extensively on "urban war zones" and the powerful influence they have on the individual child.

APPLICATIONS TO EARLY SCHOOLING

Researchers and educators need to attend not only to the codes that operate within a given system (e.g., families, schools, parents, or teachers) but also to the ways in which codes interact across systems and levels. For example, certain codes for discipline govern the regulation of child misbehavior in some contexts, for example, a home where physical punishment is acceptable) but not in others, for example, a classroom where physical punishment is not acceptable. In other cases, codes that are prescribed at the cultural level, for example, literacy or the value of an education, are inconsistent with the support provided to the child to meet the demands of these codes as enacted at lower levels, as is the case when schools are decrepit or materials outdated (Kozol, 1991). A serious question involves what happens to children when codes conflict.

In the following pages we continue the discussion of concepts from GST, using examples from early schooling when possible. The goal is to deepen familiarity with GST concepts and precipitate for the reader a shift in the metaphors used to understand and think about development and early schooling. These GST principles are equally applicable to each of the systems and subsystems in the model. They describe the behavior of systems, and in turn, the mechanisms influencing the relationships between the child/family and schooling systems.

Units of Analysis

In GST the unit of analysis is the whole. Thus the behavior of super-ordinate systems is used to explain the behavior of subordinate systems. The focus of attention and analysis is always at a level higher than the one in which the initial question is framed. For example, to understand the behavior of a teacher in the classroom, one must know something about the school, school system, and community in which they are embedded, and their relation to classroom activities. Explanation of subordinate-level activity (individual behaviors, actions of small social groups) is impossible without knowing how that activity relates to the purpose of the superordinate system (the whole). One cannot understand or explain a teacher's interactions with students without understanding how those interactions fit within and are shaped by goals (implicit or explicit) of the school, school system, or community. The superordinate system (whole) gives meaning to the activity of the subordinate system (parts).

For most of us, raised on the behaviorism that has permeated educational discourse for much of this century, the metaphor of the machine and its inherent reductionism are familiar. We have, for example, learned that we can take a complex behavior, such as reading or language acquisition, and break it down into parts through task analysis. We think this set of parts explains reading. Then we think these parts can be reassembled through teaching them, in sequence, independently, through direct instruction. Presumably when all the component parts have been learned in proper order, the ability to read or to use language has been acquired. We know now that this is not true—children do not learn to read through phonic approaches only, nor does the amount of reinforcement of phonemes or morphemes result in language acquisition. Maturationist explanations are similarly reductionistic because the individual is decontextualized.

The point is that developmental, and by implication educational, processes are holistic. Reading and language development are not reducible to an arbitrary set of component parts: complex, adaptive behavior in context cannot be broken down into component parts and learned. Systems theorists often use the metaphor of the living cell to anchor their discussions of developmental processes and concepts. The action of any part of the cell cannot be understood without reference to what the whole cell is doing: activity or functions of parts cannot be understood without reference to the whole.

These two metaphors—machine and cell—imply far different views of development. For the machine, the part is the unit of analysis. In this reductionistic view, the activity of a system can be understood completely in the activity of the parts (genes, decoding skills, time on task, socioeconomic status). Conversely, in the cell, interest is focused at the whole and interactions embedded within the whole—decoding skills as related to the use and meaning of language and print in the home and culture.

In the Contextual Systems Model, the focus is on the whole—in the case of reading difficulties, interest would be in the child's use of language and understanding of print-language connections, the child's perceptions of the meaning and use of print-language skills in the classroom and elsewhere, and phonetic skills, *but only insofar as they relate to these broader functions.* Understanding the part can only be done in reference to the activity of the whole, and the activity of the whole determines the activity of the part.

Functional Relations Between Parts and Wholes

Selecting units of analysis is complicated by the fact that systems are embedded within other systems. What is a unit in one system, for example, the child in the classroom, is also a system itself. Systems theorists discuss these transformations and relations between systems and their component units in terms of *differentiation* and *integration.*

Differentiation refers to the fact that over time, in response to internal and external pressures, one of the ways in which systems adapt is by differentiation of subunits. That is, units within the system take on different roles in order for the system as a whole to function. Conversely, integration refers to the fact that in order for the system as a whole to maintain its integrity and identity, differentiated subunits must also be integrated with one another to accomplish the primary function of the system.

In education, for example, special education and regular education (an adaptation in response to different needs of children) must be integrated within a school in order for the school to function as a whole, instead of as two separate entities within one building. This is not an argument for mainstreaming or full-inclusion, which can occur without actual integration and, perversely, can actually result in further differentiation. The point is that complex systems always experience tension between differentiation and integration. This tension is a consequence of relations between active units.

Importantly, differentiation and integration allow systems to behave efficiently. In a system in which units are both differentiated (serving different functions) and integrated (the right hand knows what the left is doing) there is a much wider variety of ways the system can adapt to pressure than if units were redundant and not connected. A system that is overly differentiated is unable to act as a whole. A system that is overly integrated is unable to respond to change.

Another concept related to the issue of functional relations between parts and wholes is *equipotentiality*. This term refers to the fact that each unit within the system has the potential to develop the properties of other units within the system, prior to differentiation. In the example cited earlier, it is conceivable that each classroom in a school has the potential of serving children with different needs, prior to the classrooms being sorted to perform this function. This lack of differentiation allows for the enormous plasticity present in early development, for example, when a child regains functional behaviors after a brain injury has destroyed the cells that once governed those functions.

Equipotentiality allows a system to recover function it would lose if a highly differentiated part was lost. Think of occasions when a highly skilled and valued staff member leaves a school. There is frequently a period of reorganization, which often entails a search for another staff member, or members, who can perform the lost function(s). To the extent that someone else in the building knows how to do what the person could do, the "recovery" period is quick. On the other hand, equipotentiality also carries redundancy, and at times inefficiency. It might not be useful for everyone in a school to be able to perform all functions.

Over-differentiation and lack of integration evident in current practices related to special education and more generally, in solutions for high-risk students. In general form, the problem occurs when a child demonstrates difficulty learning skills or has problems in behavior. This is the "pressure" to which the school, as a system, must adapt. The "solution" to this pressure usually involves a referral to an "expert" based outside the classroom, who is likely to assess highly differentiated skills and abilities—such as auditory memory or word retrieval. Intervention services are then offered that involve contact between another expert and the child, most frequently in the form of "resource" or "pull out" help in which the child's normal classroom activity is disrupted. From a systems theory perspective, such practice reflects reductionist assumptions about how children develop and how best to offer services. It also reflects a high degree of over-differentiation and specialization.

This highly differentiated approach to eligibility for and delivery of special-education services, or services for high-risk children, reflects a disintegration of the child, which itself is a negative force. The child, the skills the child brings to the classroom, the staffing of a school, and the services within the school, are all carved up under the assumption that when they are put back together, as is the case when a child is eligible and receives services, the resulting educational program reflects some functional improvement for the child. Research suggests this is not the case. Eligibility procedures (referral, assessment, labeling) are extremely costly to schools; the assessment procedures conducted and services offered often have little connection to the skills the child needs in order to perform competently in the "regular" classroom (Ysseldyke et al., 1983). It is not surprising that many children referred into the special-education system never come out (Singer & Butler 1987). In sum, the functional benefit of many of these activities appears to be the removal of the child from the regular classroom. In some cases this may be needed. The point is that this response to children's varied needs is over-differentiated and, from a systems view, exemplifies a dysfunctional organization. Differentiation without integration is characteristic of inflexible systems. Equipotentiality is a characteristic of highly flexible systems.

These principles are also reflected in observations we have made in school buildings. In a study conducted by one of us, we observed a child playing in the housekeeping corner of a classroom using very rich language to narrate play and interact with other children. In the midst of this rich language interaction the speech pathologist entered the room, removed the child from the play context without attending at all to the activity occurring, and began practicing the "s" sound with the child. In this particular instance the classroom context and speech intervention context were *not* viewed as equipotential when in fact they probably were, with respect to language development.

In another example, about half of the children in the kindergarten classroom of one of our daughters were what would be referred to as "at-risk" children. This classroom had a very skilled teacher, an aide, and about 18 children. The daily schedule was pinned next to the door and reflected the comings and goings of children in the room. Guess which children moved the most? Guess which children were having the most difficulty, according to the teacher, adapting to the classroom routine? Guess which children spent the most time in the classroom? Guess how much time the teacher had to spend managing transitions? One boy identified as one of the most "at-risk" children in the classroom came and went more than three times a day, going to "services" that were in addition to the other extra services offered to all the children, such as music, art, and gym. This child probably spent more time in the hallway than in the classroom.

Motivation

Systems theory differs from reductionist perspectives in terms of the locus of developmental change and the organism's motivation to change. Within reductionistic behavioral perspectives, developmental change, and motivation to change, is derived extrinsically—from being acted on. The best example of this is behavioral psychology's view of learning, especially language acquisition, in which children perform behaviors or acquire new skills, as a function of the contingencies present in the environment, namely the delivery of positive (or negative) reinforcement. Maturationist views of change are just as narrow, except that the locus of developmental change is the unfolding of genetic programs, viewed largely within the frame of chronological age. In both cases the organism (the child) is a passive participant in change—change is something that happens to the child, whether from within or without.

GST views motivation as intrinsic to the system (the child) and inherent in the fact that systems are active. Developmental change follows as a consequence of the activity and evolution of interacting systems. The child is *inherently active*: constructing meaning, adapting, seeking challenges, practicing emergent capacities. This is a much different view of the child than the passive child who is acted on by contingencies, or the equally passive child whose behaviors are pre-programmed. Furthermore, the child adapts within contexts that are dynamic and fluid, always variable. Motivation, or the "desire" to change, is derived from the co-action of systems: of child and context.

Change, or development, of systems occurs regardless of the nature of the "input" variables in this process. In other words, children will learn regardless of whether they are reinforced, or whether they are "old enough." Children will acquire skills that facilitate their adaptation. In some cases, these may be skills that enable them to be thrown out of school so that they can engage the street economy. In other cases, these can be skills that enable them to disengage from an overwhelming classroom with excessive demands for coping (e.g., the boy with three transitions in and out of the classroom each morning).

In GST, motivation and activity are synonymous; an active organism interacting with a context will learn (or adapt or change) over time. GST does not disregard the fact that some extrinsic contingencies guide the performance of behavior and influence the acquisition of certain behaviors, and that development of some behavioral systems (such as written language, or formal mathematics) is mediated by external input (e.g., Resnick, 1995). But, the motivation of any system can only be understood within the larger, superordinate system. Individuals' motivation to become literate occurs within the support for literacy in the immediate and larger culture. Motivation to change is seen not as inside or outside the system but as integrated into its basic properties. The evidence for children's intuitive use of higher-order mathematics skills and concepts in the absence of formal instruction (Resnick, 1995; Rogoff, 1990) clearly demonstrates that motivation, even for academic skills, is not dependent on formal schooling. Ironically, children are often better intuitive mathematicians before formal instruction than after.

Assumptions about the locus of change and motivation have fundamental consequences for the organization of schools and delivery of instruction. Views of motivation as externally located and change as a function of input to the child will inevitably result in instruction that is teacher-dominated, driven by curricular scope and sequence charts, behavioral objectives, and drill and practice—which are the dominant modes of instruction in the United States (Stevenson & Lee, 1990). Biological views of motivation result in "developmental" or "transitional" grades that serve to delay entry into formal schooling in the hope that a year of maturation will help the child catch up to his or her chronologically aged peers, these views of motivation have been singularly ineffective (Graue, 1993; Shepard & Smith, 1989; Walsh et al., 1992).

A view of the child as an active participant in learning and a belief that developmental change will occur regardless of input lead to seeing instruction as facilitation. Teachers pose challenges and guide activity toward adapting to those challenges. Interestingly, these styles of instruction are present in Asian countries that we often seek to emulate (Stevenson & Lee, 1990). From this perspective classrooms and teachers look very different from how they have in the past.

Change
GST and reductionistic views differ also with respect to how change is conceptualized and assessed. In reductionistic views, change is a function of acquiring or adding new parts or skills—progression from two-word sentences to three-word sentences or learning more letters in the alphabet. In GST, change is often viewed as discontinuous and qualitative. It occurs when systems reorganize and transform under

pressure to adapt. In this context, change is not the acquisition of skills or the addition of new units to an existing repertoire but a reorganization of relations among units (old and new) within the system. Therefore change is indexed by level of organization (simple to complex, differentiated vs. undifferentiated, integrated vs. nonintegrated).

Self-stabilization and adaptive self-reorganization refer to GST principles describing both stability and adaptive change of a complex system. *Self-stabilization* refers to the gyroscopic property of complex systems in which the system can respond to perturbations or demands while not reorganizing in response to this demand. The system responds by rearranging internal dynamics or relations and adapts to pressure without altering its basic structure or identity. Self-stabilization is a very important property of systems. It preserves their identity in the face of contextual pressures or demands, and insures that major change, or reorganization, occurs at a slow, regulated pace. If it were not for self-stabilization, the behavior of systems, and individuals, would be wildly unpredictable and unstable.

Take, for example, the challenges of entering school for the first time. The child who resists change in this unfamiliar context of school is frequently seen as having a problem, or being a problem. In fact, the real problem would be if in this situation she or he readily changed in response to all the new demands.

Adaptive self-reorganization refers to the response of a complex system to a more constant or intense environmental (or internal) pressure or demand. In this process the self-stabilizing properties of the system are inadequate to meet the demands placed on them, and the system must reorganize in order to respond adaptively. Small calibrations, of the self-stabilizing type, are inadequate for the system to function with respect to this new challenge.

The failure of self-stabilizing forces to respond adaptively to a challenge is a turning point in the development of a system because failure to reorganize may spell the "death" of the system. Systems that do not adaptively reorganize basically do not change in any meaningful way. It can be said that they are not evolving and that they have become rigid (having only one response to any problem). This can happen to individuals as well as larger systems, for example, schools. The calls for reform, or for "real change" in the schools, are in large part a response to the perceived increase in high-risk children, and an example of the need for adaptive self-reorganization. It is recognized that small calibrations of the type that have already been used (incremental change) will not address these challenges.

Thus there are several mechanisms by which systems change in response to internal and external pressures. As noted previously, development of systems occurs as a consequence of interaction: a system comes in contact with context, and contact produces development, that is, change. Coming into contact with context is a necessity—no system can exist except in a system. Contact always occurs, and systems make innumerable micro-responses to contact in a constant process of self-stabilization. Internal triggers (e.g., genes, history of development, etc.) may precipitate other responses by the system.

Reorganization takes place as the system accumulates a pattern of self-stabilizing responses to internal or external pressures of this constant-contact sort. Also, reorganization takes place in response to external pressures of sufficient intensity or duration to make the "usual" self-stabilizing response inadequate. Change of complex systems takes time and does not usually come about by large, one-time reorganizations following large external challenges (such as is sought by most educational reformers) but by incremental changes within subsystems that are constantly adapting to the demands of contact with other systems. That is one reason why time is an explicit variable in the Model.

Systems and subsystems interact in a dynamic flow of activity and change. Subsystems (e.g., child-peer) interact across larger systems (child-home, child-school), and as a consequence, these larger systems (child-home, child-school) often are pressured to reorganize to accommodate changes in the subsystems (child-peer). For example, as any parent knows, once a child begins to develop strong peer relationships outside the home, these relationships affect child-parent relations within the home.

A relevant example is seen in the influx of high-risk children into the schools. As teachers found it more difficult to teach and interact with children in their classrooms, and classrooms became increasingly populated with children needing "different" interactions, schools began to consider reform and reorganization in response to these demands of subordinate systems. One of us has observed the growth of an early childhood center that serves at-risk and special-needs children over the past few years. As it has grown, change has been incremental, and of the sort typically followed in schools. The school added new staff, until the adult-child ratio has decreased to almost 1:2.5. The staff added have been primarily specialists, for example, speech therapists, social workers, occupational therapists, school psychologists, as opposed to generalists, that is, classroom teachers. This was the response of the school to the perception that children coming into the school had more needs than children entering previously. The perceived "imbalance" in the system (the influx of at-risk children), and the "failure" of teachers and classrooms to solve this problem resulted in, over time, the school's being reorganized in much more complex, highly differentiated structure, requiring considerable efforts at organization and communication functions. Other responses could have been possible, for example, more classroom teachers, or more teacher assistants.

Time

Finally the role of time as an input variable in the change process is recognized explicitly in the developmental systems approach. Action and change take place with time as a fundamental component, or put more directly, they take place in time. Time will influence the extent or degree of change, even with all else equal. Almost all models of schooling or education have no code for time as an input variable. Thus, researchers count how many times some event occurs, but generally ignore the relationship of these events across time. When a child does something, when he or she does it in relation to other actions or events, and how these actions change in relation to other actions or events across time are likely to be more important in understanding her or his learning than how often she or he performs a particular skill. So we count the number of practice arithmetic computations a child does instead of watching how she or he uses arithmetic in daily life problems (Resnick, 1995).

In fact, the very meaning of an action is likely to be different from the beginning of a school year to later in that year. For example, a punch that is aggressive or defensive in the first week of school will be playful and affectionate in February. A graduate student working with one of us was doing a study of children in an after-school program. She asked a third grader what a friend was. The young boy looked at her like she was daft to be asking such a dumb question and replied, "Someone who steps on the back of your shoes or punches you in line"—actions that researchers count as "aggression events."

Researchers have continued to ignore the effect of time in spite of the fact that it is widely recognized that children learn at different rates and that systems change slowly (Boulding, 1985). We are not referring here to the concept of graded instruction or that children change grades from year to year as an index of time as an input. We are suggesting that time is a variable, and that change, within systems, is in part a function of time. In almost all models of education time is a constant, or at best, a variable that must be controlled. For example, in most classrooms, instruction takes place in "lessons" that are embedded within "units." Exposure to information is controlled through the number of lessons (or units), and most frequently, when a lesson or unit is "finished" the instructor moves on to another (hopefully related) lesson (unit). Americans do not, as the Asians do, work until mastery is achieved, regardless of the time (Stevenson & Lee, 1990).

At another level, time is almost not considered at all. School reform efforts to improve academic achievement are often allowed a "year or two" by the school board, state department, or funding agency, in which to demonstrate effectiveness. We have both been involved in efforts to evaluate programs for high-risk 4-year-olds that (a) involve intervention for roughly a 9-month period, and (b) are expected to show effects after the first year or be threatened with losing funding. Both of these assumptions of program implementation and evaluation fail to consider time as key variable. If anything has been learned from the early-intervention evaluation literature, it is that programs need time to fine-tune themselves and work effectively, and that generally, the length of time in program is the best predictor of program effectiveness (e.g., Ramey & Campbell, 1991). The change mechanisms of self-reorganization and self-stabilization take place with time as an explicit input variable.

Prediction and Assessment

Educators spend a lot of time and energy wrestling with the problem of predictability, usually in the context of assessing children's skills or progress. It is fundamental to education in the United States that judgments are made about "educational levels" in order to predict the likelihood of success (or failure) on a subsequent task. GST and mechanistic models of development differ with respect to the extent to which complete predictability can be achieved. In reductionistic models (behavioral or maturationist), predicting the activity or behavior of the organism (machine) is viewed as possible, and near perfect predictability achievable once "measures are better and more reliable." This particular assumption has driven a great deal of research and theory on child development over the last 40 years. In fact, most research on behavioral development implicitly assumes that future outcomes can and should be predicted, and with better measures, improved (and near perfect) prediction can be achieved.

A corollary point mentioned earlier is that reductionist views assume that prediction is linear and that developmental change can be reduced to an algorithm that translates development at Time 1 into development at Time 2. The achievement of near-perfect predictability as a possible goal is completely consistent with a view of the organism as reducible to parts and developmental change being a function of acquiring different and new parts. In this view prediction is a function of accurate measurement at both times and an estimate of the rate of change.

Within a GST perspective, perfect predictability is recognized as impossible; all prediction is probabilistic. Recalling that living systems are active and that the behavior one tries to predict is part of this activity, GST recognizes that attempts to measure activity are largely artificial; relations between assessments (correlations and validity coefficients) are of necessity bounded. Estimates of abilities, skills, or future performance will *never* approach 1.0, not because measures are unreliable but because the complex, dynamic systems are active, hence actual description of them in static terms can never be more than an estimate. GST also posits that the interrelated and complex behaviors of systems transforms the system over time, such that new and different organizations govern the system's activity, making prediction over time even more difficult. In physics, this problem has been addressed by the Heisenberg Uncertainly Principle—it is accepted that one can never completely estimate the behavior of an active system.

Recently economists, historians, and paleontologists have struggled with the problem of incomplete explanation or prediction. Economists can make only broad judgments about the likelihood of certain types of activity in the economy, and meteorologists are inaccurate in predicting weather, because not all relevant factors can be known a priori and because random events occur. In these fields change and prediction are seen in light of the concept of *emergents*. Emergents are what occur when systems reorganize in light of new adaptational challenges; the actual nature of an emergent is unpredictable, but that a new form of organization will emerge is entirely predictable.

In the GST context, change is viewed as qualitative, not quantitative. Causality is circular; the existence of multiple feedback loops between different parts of a system makes it impossible to predict the behavior of the system (or any part) based on knowledge of the system's (or the parts') behavior at a previous time. Measurement, in this perspective, can never be more than a snapshot or slice of activity, and is therefore a very indirect, and inherently imperfect, representation of the activity to predict. In this sense, GST posits that prediction is not possible and that the only "forecasting statements" possible about the behavior of complex systems are probability statements. This is not to say that one cannot make reasonably strong predictions about the likelihood of certain outcomes and events in a system, for example, schooling. Systems are not chaotic—it is the highly *patterned* nature of interactions within a system that makes a system a system.

Good teachers can easily identify the children who will likely have difficulty in school; they intuitively understand relationships in school, or in the worst case, they can have a lot to do with predicted negative outcomes. For example, research on transition or developmental programs shows children who are predicted to be not ready for school are placed in programs where they are effectively ignored for a year (e.g., Shepard & Smith, 1989; Walsh et al., 1992). Some variables are easily described and do have strong links to outcomes, however, when the ability to predict is equated with interpretations of linear causality (because this child is dressed poorly and dirty then he will not learn; because this child has difficulty sitting still he has an attention-deficit disorder and belongs in a different classroom), then we fall into the trap of thinking the perceived cause and outcome are *always* linked. Self-fulfilling prophecies are basically a result of using "good" predictive data in a causal manner, thus narrowing the field of opportunity. It is easy to organize schooling so that only certain individuals will succeed, but that says a lot about the organizational skills of educators and little about the children who fail.

Do We Create Our Own Problems?

From a systems notion, there is *dialectic* among systems, or between the organism and context, with each influencing the other and having to subsequently adapt to the change created in the other. This dialectic is seen in the tension between humans and the contexts they create for themselves, and between individual children and the contexts with which they interact. Human beings are, as Weber noted, suspended in webs of significance that they have spun.

At the societal level, we are particularly concerned about the effects of "unplanned national experiments." These are widespread changes that ripple through society absent any explicit agenda and without mechanisms in place to monitor effects. What, for example, are the effects of: (1) the restructuring of American families into more dispersed and fragmented units; (2) increasing violence and the apparent acceptance or, at least, tolerance thereof; (3) increased reliance on medication as a solution to life problems? We raise these as examples of ways in which contemporary American society has created new contexts that present challenges to the rearing of healthy children. When cultures create constraints or variations for which there is no biological, or for that matter, cultural capacity to adapt by individuals or the group, then there can be a serious problem.

Although society is being dramatically altered, schools appear to be changing little if at all (Romberg & Price, 1983; Sirotnik, 1983). Right now, at the level of school systems, a major dialectic is being played out with respect to the extent to which children with disabilities will be included in regular classroom activities. Most now agree that the solution of previous generations to institutionalize or dramatically exclude these children from the mainstream is inconsistent with the values of a democratic society. The mainstreaming trends of the 1970s were a result of the first wave of inclusion efforts. Predictably, the new "integrated" contexts challenged educators, and in many cases led to renewed efforts to see more exclusive placements as appropriate, hence the growth of day treatment and self-contained placements in the 1980s. Now, armed with strengthened civil rights legislation, advocates have renewed the call for all children to be included in mainstream education. In each case, change brings about new demands on the system.

At the level of the individual child, dialectic interaction is seen in the constant transactions that occur between child and environment and the changes in each that occur over time. Children are not only being affected by policy changes, they are affecting those who work with them. The research literature on the child's effects on the caregiver attests to the fact that children have a considerable effect on the adults with whom they interact, and dialectically, they in turn must adapt to the consequences of the changes they make in parent practices and beliefs.

Assessing the "Health" of Systems

Finally, GST analysis suggests a set of principles for the assessment of systems: a set of variables on which systems differ that index the degree of health or fitness of a given system to respond to challenge or to regulate the behavior of individuals (subsystems) organized within the system. We will rely heavily on these principles for the analysis of educational efforts to address the needs of young children entering school, and will profile school and educational contexts with respect to these principles.

The capacity of a system to adapt is the main "developmental" task of systems. Systems that adapt are those that develop, whereas those that do not adapt often perish or languish. From this perspective flexibility is a hallmark of systemic health or capacity to adapt. A *flexible system* is able to respond to a wide range of contextual conditions and internal pressures.

Another aspect of systems that can be evaluated is the extent of differentiation present. Earlier examples contrasted the positive benefits of equipotentiality with the negative consequences of highly differentiated systems. Although many systems theorists argue that developing systems are increasingly differentiated, and that differentiation should be viewed positively, we argue that highly flexible, plastic contexts/systems are desirable for handling the needs of immature or highly variable organisms. Under these circumstances, less differentiation may be better.

In any case, to the extent that differentiation occurs, it must be accompanied by integration of the differentiated parts in order for the health of the whole to be maintained. The advantages of differentiation largely occur in efficiency (a "part" accomplishes something the "whole" used to do), but without integration, it is very easy for fragmentation and isolation of function to occur. Soon the integrity of the system is compromised. One important reason why less differentiation is desirable in schools is that the "solution" to the majority of school "problems" (including those of high-risk kids) has been to increase differentiation: add specialists, give the child a special class or program. All of these lead to fragmentation of the child's experience. Overcompensating toward less-differentiated solutions is a direction for consideration; insuring integration within highly differentiated solutions is essential.

Systems can also be evaluated with respect to feedback functions. Again, the interrelated nature of systems requires a large number of feedback loops through which information is transmitted. If feedback is not prompt and accurate, then the activity of the system is delayed, distorted, or compromised. Feedback tends to be very slow in overly differentiated systems, and distorted when systems lack regular linkages. For these reasons we introduced the notion of conversation as a metaphor for linkages within and across systems that serve feedback functions. A good conversation is what Bruner calls a "transaction," that is, it is "premised on a mutual sharing of assumptions and beliefs about how the world is, how the mind works, what we are up to, and how communication should proceed" (1987, p. 81). Like good conversation, feedback loops should be transactional—they should "listen" to the message and share enough meaning to understand the message. The message should serve to increase shared meaning, so that the "listener" can calibrate behavior accordingly.

There are not enough examples of widespread good conversations occurring in the systems surrounding young children's transitions to school. When good conversation occurs, regulation is a natural product. Without conversation, regulation is difficult or missing. Risk is reflected in the nature of the conversation. When the conversation is bad, risk is high.

Case Study: *Gary*

Gary is a six-year-old boy in the first grade. He is having considerable difficulty with social relations and impulse control, and is not performing any preacademic-type skills in the classroom. His mother also reports problems with his behavior at home. Gary's mother is well-educated, divorced from Gary's father, and has lived with Gary in her sister's home for the past two years. Gary's mother is very involved with his school progress and has worked closely with the kindergarten and first-grade teachers, who describe her as supportive of and cooperative with their efforts.

Gary was the product of a planned and uncomplicated pregnancy. He is described by his mother as a good baby who was somewhat precocious; he crawled and walked early for his age. Gary's mother and father were divorced just prior to his entering kindergarten at age four-and-a-half. Gary blamed himself for his parent's divorce, and his mother sought counseling services for him, although he continues to wish for his parents to reunite.

Gary's father did not see him for three months after the divorce, and remarried six months after the divorce. He rarely sees Gary, and Gary and his mother recently moved from the city in which the family lived together prior to the divorce to live with her sister and be nearer to her other siblings. Gary's mother is attempting to reestablish a business as a stock broker and travels outside of the country for four to five days a month, with trips arranged on very short notice. Adjustment to the present living situation at her sister's is difficult for Gary and his mother. Family members perceive Gary as difficult and his mother as coddling. The mother perceives family members as interfering with her efforts to parent in difficult circumstances.

Gary's mother grew up near where she currently lives and is the second of ten children. She describes her family as close. Both her parents are deceased. All siblings live within the same geographical area and are in frequent contact with each other. When Gary's mother was 16, her mother was hospitalized for depression and died 5 years later of cancer at the age of 42. Gary's mother's father was an alcoholic who remarried a woman with six children with adjustment problems; the marriage ended within one year. During the second marriage Gary's mother lived out of the home with an older sibling and assumed custody of the younger siblings.

Gary's adjustment to school has been problematic. He reportedly has difficulty sitting still and attending for more than a few minutes at a time. He is referred for and placed in special education and receives resource help in reading in first grade. Gary is less involved with neighborhood children than he used to be. He seeks out old friends less frequently and spends more time around the house. Gary's mother reports him to be caring and adultlike toward her, "like a best friend." Others describe him as manipulative toward her and excessively dependent.

In school Gary is frequently out of control, lying on the floor screaming, refusing to do schoolwork, and isolating himself from friends. Gary is seen for evaluation by a psychologist who notes his above-average abilities, tendencies to seek control in relationships, and excessive dependency and manipulation of his mother. Mother is viewed as anxious about Gary's independence and encouraging of his immaturity.

A plan is developed between mother, school (special educator), and psychologist to address Gary's needs. Special education is offered in a full-time self-contained class for children with behavior problems, in which the emphasis is on consistent responses and expectations for performance, with contingencies for appropriate and inappropriate behavior. Gary is seen by a psychologist, who emphasizes establishing communication, expressing anxiety and emotion, and understanding of his experiences. Gary's mother is also seen by a psychologist who emphasizes supporting her independence from siblings, encouraging autonomy in her son, establishing limits for Gary's behavior, and identifying age-appropriate activities for Gary. All professionals are in monthly contact.

After four months Gary expresses strong interest in peers, joins the Cub Scouts, is exhibiting appropriate behavior in school, and is performing above expected levels on academic skills. Gary and his mother engage in appropriate arguments and exhibit good problem solving. Mother is reportedly moving out of her sister's home and is planning to marry a man she has been dating. Gary is placed back in the regular classroom where a six month follow-up shows excellent progress.

Where is risk located in this system and what were probable consequences of this risk? What was the functional benefit of special education? What processes account for Gary's success?

6

The Child As a Developing System

Child development plays a central role in the Contextual Systems Model. No understanding of the relationship between the child/family and schooling systems can be understood without reference to developmental processes in the child. Thus, *child development, within the context of the child/family and schooling relationship,* is the central unit of analysis in educational discourse—not the culture, family, school, classroom, or teacher/lesson. The majority of reform efforts fail to recognize this fact. Instead these efforts focus attention on specific facets of this relationship or the subordinate systems without understanding how these facets affect the development of the child. Without central consideration of the child within the relationship of child/family and school, and recognition that school is a context for the child developing (for better or worse) within this relationship, reform efforts can easily run counter to the needs of the children they intend to serve. This chapter presents a more detailed discussion of the Contextual Systems Model view of child development.

A DEVELOPMENTAL PERSPECTIVE
Developing children are *open systems.* Many interrelated parts and processes weave together in the developing child. These processes and parts, by themselves, do not describe the child. Intelligence, social competence, aggressive behavior, time on task, or learning style do not describe the child. That is the "systems" part of the premise. Open

systems are in dynamic exchange with the contexts in which they find themselves (Ford & Ford, 1987). Child systems exchange information, material, energy, and activity with other systems within various contexts. In this process of exchange, the child changes and develops—self-regulation and self-reorganization occur in this way.

This dynamic interplay, or exchange process, between child and context cannot easily be "stopped" and "evaluated." This is the task of many assessment instruments, by which performance in some "part" of the child is measured. Thus intelligence (or readiness) tests examine only one aspect of the child as a system, and they tend to measure static products, not the processes by which the construct (e.g., intelligence) might be expressed in context. Systems are best evaluated at a holistic level, the level at which parts are organized (Greenspan & Greenspan, 1991). Sroufe (1989) and others argue that better indices for examining development are patterns of adaptation to salient developmental challenges. Performance on intelligence tests may be a useful indicator for some purposes but a more useful indicator might be how the child uses available resources (their own and those in their environment: social, cognitive, and personal) to solve real-world problems in the classroom context. Resnick's (1994) studies of children's development of mathematics skills clearly support this view of evaluation.

Adaptation refers to the relational, dynamic properties of development, and reflects the role that context plays in the performance of any given behavior. Context provides input to the activity of the child as a developing system—it constrains activity, challenges existing structures and capacities, and "prods" the system to new levels of organization. How the system responds to this input is the essential feature of adaptation. Adaptation is a molar construct that involves all aspects of the child as a developing system—emotions; cognitive processes such as memory, planning, and creativity; motivation; social and interactive behavior; communication; and movement. Adaptation can also be described in terms of its quality—do observed behavior patterns foster the child's adjustment and fit in a variety of situations?

Child As System
Although development proceeds in differentiated areas, development across various areas is integrated; motor development affects cognitive and social development and vice versa. In this way, various components of developmental capacity are linked with one another. In a developing system, integration of component units also proceeds with

differentiation of units. Greenspan (1989) suggests two key areas in which differentiation occurs: the *modes of adaptation* and the *goals of adaptation*. Modes of adaptation refers to the capacities/skills at the child's disposal that can be mobilized to adapt to a particular challenge. For example, the infant has very few modes within her behavioral repertoire to use in the service of adaptation; she can cry or smile. For the four-year-old, language, cognitive-delay strategies, symbolic expression in play, and direct discharge of feelings are all available for adaptive use.

Goals of adaptation refer to the orientation of the developing system to accomplish certain "tasks" in order to achieve a comfortable degree of "fit." As development proceeds, the complexity of the child's relationships with context also increases—the infant has fairly reflexive, homeostatic interactions around feeding, sleeping, and needing stimulation in which the goal is some degree of regulation of physical tension and arousal. The four-year-old's interactions with its context are organized around elaboration of a symbol system, mastery of the object world in increasingly complex ways, and regulation of behavior in peer context, all of which involve complex, multipurpose relationships with context.

Notions of development within the Contextual Systems Model extend beyond simple linear notions of change and of static, traitlike conceptualizations of child outcome or development. These constructs find favor in mechanistic, reductionistic views of behavior and development, frequently offered in behaviorist or maturationist theories. The focus within these perspectives on traitlike characteristics and individual behaviors results in simplistic notions of how change occurs. In the Contextual Systems Model development is viewed as the changing organization of a system, a series of reorganizations of systemic activity patterns in response to challenges. Children seek increasingly complex stimuli and challenges that are consonant with their capacity to adapt, and these in turn shape adaptation. Conversely, contexts respond to patterns of child adaptation with new challenges. This process operates consistently with the principles of adaptive self-reorganization and self-regulation described in the previous chapter. In short, a constant process of co-action between child and context gives rise to increasingly diverse and complex modes of adapting on the part of the developmental system, in this case the child. These modes of adaptation, increasingly complex and differentiated over time, are cast in many theories as key developmental themes that frame the specific components of adaptation at a given phase or period.

The Role of Context in Child Adaptation

Contexts can be described, in relation to their role in facilitating or impeding adaptation, in terms of their *affordance value*. High affordance contexts are those that are rich in resources keyed to the child's developmental status. Low affordance contexts may be those in which few resources exist, or whatever resources do exist are not well matched to the child's developmental capacities. Contextual resources are intimately involved in the child's adaptational patterns. In this way, adaptation is *distributed* (Resnick, 1991, 1994). Resnick defines distributed in relation to cognitive processes in this way:

> Under normal circumstances, mental activity involves social coordination with others. What makes an individual competent is not just what he or she knows but also how his or her knowledge fits with that of others with whom activity must be coordinated...activity is shared with tools...and with physical material. Thus there is a distribution of cognitive work not only among people but also between people and tools.... The tools embody a portion of the intelligence that is needed to accomplish a particular task. (p. 476)

Similarly, but at a more global level, we argue that adaptation is distributed, in the sense that the actual competence of a child to adapt to a certain challenge involves resources within the child, the situation(s) in which the challenge occurs, and the relation of the child to the challenge and the situation(s). Keating (in press) describes the role of context as "setting the external constraints that limit and shape the actual self-organization that takes place" (p. 12). The Contextual Systems Model views the role of context as even more essential—unable to be separated from what the child is perceiving, doing, knowing, feeling, understanding. The child as system and context as system(s) are separated by a highly permeable boundary. Adaptation is distributed across these systems.

The notion of adaptation as distributed across child and context—or across systems noted in the model presented earlier, is radically different from the view taken in most approaches to schooling, especially for children with high-risk coefficients. In the Contextual Systems Model it makes no sense whatsoever to think about "*child* readiness for school" without a clear understanding of the ways in which child adaptation is facilitated or impeded by family and schooling contexts. Nor does it make sense to assess "readiness" by asking the child to perform isolated, preacademic tasks. These will simply not be a valid index of the nature of the child's capacity to adapt. The distributed nature of adaptation requires a broader, more flexible lens.

Developmental Themes

Many theorists describe somewhat different themes for different periods and domains of development (e.g., Erickson, 1968; Greenspan, 1989; Piaget, 1970; Sroufe, 1989). For the most part these themes have contributed to structuralist notions of development and reinforced stage theories of development. In Sroufe's view, these themes are salient developmental challenges that give meaning to observation of child adaptation. They are not stages through which all children pass. Instead, the Contextual Systems Model uses these themes not as descriptors of stages but as reflecting levels of organization in developing systems (Greenspan, 1989). Over developmental time, patterns of adaptation to earlier developmental challenges are organized within adaptation to subsequent challenges: early adaptation lays the foundation for subsequent competence. Themes from infancy through early childhood are discussed below.

The first challenge involves *regulation and modulation of physiological arousal.* The infant (and caregiver) must tolerate increasingly complex physical and social stimulation and maintain an organized state in the face of increasing arousal. Cycles of sleep and alertness, feeding and arousal all begin to become organized very early on within this period. The immature status of the newborn predisposes the child to require caregiver interactions to help maintain organization in the face of cyclic variations (Hofer, 1994; Sander, 1975). The competent infant in this phase adapts to routines set by caregivers and, with caregivers, establishes regular rhythms of feeding, activity/alertness, and sleep. High affordance contexts insure the maintenance of smooth, regular, predictable routines and practices that are contingent on infant cues. In this interaction context the infant and caregiver mesh interactive behaviors to establish these routines. Over time, the patterns broaden to include interactive play and form a behavioral matrix that organizes the infant in the face of increasingly complex stimulation—the definition of the competent infant.

Low affordance contexts give rise to over- and under-arousal—the infant who shows little or no predictability in terms of routines, who shows little interest in interactions, or who is so difficult to settle and soothe that caregivers become increasingly stressed and either inconsistent or unresponsive.

The *formation of an effective attachment relationship* flows from patterns of interactions established around physiological and emotional regulation by the caregiver. Defined as the affective bond between child and caregiver, an effective attachment affords the child a sense of security in the context of a relationship, and provides a basis within this relationship for exploration of the object and interpersonal world. Key roles for the co-activity of child and context with respect to formation of an effective attachment relationship involve adult responsiveness, emotional availability, and development of an effective signaling system.

In a secure attachment relationship, the child develops a sense of the caregiver as available under conditions of stress or threat. The child comes to rely on the presence of the caregiver as an effective comfortor of distress and seeks the caregiver purposefully under these conditions (Ainsworth, Blehar, Waters, & Wall, 1978). The caregiver must have the capacity to read and respond to the child's cues without distortion. This capacity is affected by the caregiver's previous attachment experiences and own self-regulation of attention and emotion (Fonagy, Steele, & Steele, 1991; Main & Hesse, 1990). Ineffective attachment relationships, or incompetent patterns of adaptation to the attachment "challenge," are manifest through avoidance of the caregiver, ambivalence to the caregiver, and confused/disorganized behavior when interacting with the caregiver (Cassidy, 1994). Attachment processes have been shown to be salient features around which child-caregiver and child-adult interactions are organized throughout infancy and early childhood (Crittenden, 1992; Greenberg, Cicchetti, & Cummings, 1990).

During the toddler-preschooler period, *effective self-reliance or autonomy (object mastery, active problem solving, motivation)* emerges as a theme around which development is organized. Effective self-reliance emphasizes that the child enthusiastically engages problems in the world, persists in using his or her own efforts to address the problem, and before giving up or becoming frustrated, the child signals for resources, and uses those resources from others to solve the problem. Building on the effective attachment relationship developed within the previous phase, the caregiver-child dyad now uses the child's exploratory forays and the caregiver's provision of comfort to regulate the child's behavior at a distance, in exploratory situations. Knowing the caregiver will be available when distressed, the child is free to move about the world and focus attention on learning about the properties of objects, places, and people. Without that knowledge the child remains focused on either obtaining the caregiver's assistance, insuring their availability (dependency), or exploring in an overly independent fashion, not being able to make use of the caregiver as a resource to help when the inevitable frustrations, impediments to exploration, or dangers arise, as they will with every two-year-old. Self-reliance at this phase of development is not equivalent to simple, commonly used notions of independence that involve the child's solo behavior. Instead self-reliance refers to the child's motivation to explore, persistence in the face of frustration, and effective use of adults as resources whom these children are able to effectively integrate into their exploratory behaviors. Interestingly, the children classified as having avoidant attachment strategies, who can easily be mistaken for being independent because they tend not to be distressed on separation, have been shown to be greater risk-takers, more accident prone, less persistent, and less successful explorers (Lieberman, 1992).

An expanded ability to organize and coordinate environmental and personal resources becomes important as demands on the child become increasingly complex. Flexibility, and an increasing capacity to modulate arousal using relational and self resources, becomes a key factor in competent adaptation to future developmental issues (Thompson, 1994). A key feature of competent adaptation at this level, noted primarily by Greenspan (1989), is the development of an *emerging representational capacity*. Symbols, gesture, and early language forms are used to mediate child-context interactions. Crying becomes differentiated and purposive; words and sentences can be substituted for behavior in the expression of emotion, intent, needs, comfort, or goals. Bowlby (1969) also discusses this as a phase in which a goal-corrected partnership emerges. The child and parent (adult) negotiate contact using symbols; goals and plans mesh (Bowlby, 1969). The emergence of a representational capacity is a fundamental shift in development, in which experience is no longer coded only directly in behavior, but indirectly in symbols.

This new capacity, after it consolidates and extends into new behavioral domains, will provide the foundation for sophisticated language, reading, self-control mechanisms, new levels of cognitive processing, friendships (perspective-taking and other forms of social cognition), and other higher-order functions.

The period of emergent representational capacity is a critical period for context, and frequently problems in development in the toddler-preschool period can be traced to contextual affordances for representation. The role of context in supporting competent adaptation is very tricky. The child begins to use symbols in ways that are prized and valued by caregivers and others in his or her world—language, self-control, planning, meshing of goals and plans. But recall that adaptation at this phase—the use of symbols—is distributed. It remains completely dependent on context, and the nature of the situational variables in which the broad developmental challenge is cast.

This phase of development is also critical for the transition to school. Almost everything a child is called on to do in school rests on the successful emergence, extension, and consolidation of representational capacities. Focused attention, language, peer relations, communication, reading, higher-order thinking and problem solving, social cognition, appropriate use of adults, and above all, self-control, emerge from this kernel of representational capacity. Incompetent patterns of adaptation to earlier developmental challenges (physiological regulation, attachment, exploration) undermines developing effective representational skills. In turn, even for children with a prior history of competent adaptation, the challenges of symbolic exchanges with context are serious enough to suggest that many children develop problems related to this phase (Greenberg, Kusche, & Speltz, 1990).

In the late preschool years, *effective peer relations* are a central issue of concern. Peers are sources of challenges and resources for the child from preschool age on, and the child must learn to integrate affiliative systems with competition, mastery, and increasingly abstract and representational forms of information. Many authors argue that peer relations form even earlier than the late preschool years, and that peer interactions play an important role in regulating behavior in contexts, such as day-care and preschool (Sroufe, 1983). Parker and Asher (1987) established the importance of peer relations for later development in a comprehensive review of peer relations studies, concluding that the quality of peer relations is a major indicator of developmental competence in social and emotional development, and a critical indicator of success in schools.

Although many children coming to school have had substantial opportunities to establish peer relations in the preschool years, through day care and other contexts, in school the peer opportunities widen and are more challenging. Adult-child ratios drop dramatically as children enter school, from 1:10 in most child-care settings to ratios in many primary grade classrooms of 1:20 and higher. Children are much more on their own in establishing peer interactions in school. Consequently, without adult assistance to mediate peer relations, competence in peer interactions is a function of co-regulation between child and peer contexts. For these reasons, early experience, self-control, social development, and other factors related to prior adaptation become increasingly important factors in predicting the success of children in the peer arena in school.

Formation of a sense of self, effective self-control, and symbolic exchange are the hallmarks of adaptation in early childhood and the key elements of adapting to challenges for cognitive/academic achievement, cooperation in social groups, and the beginnings of a sense of identity. Greenspan (1989) suggests that by the late preschool/ elementary school ages, children's adaptation is a function of fairly sophisticated representational processes. Children manipulate language, symbols, and internal representations (images, etc.), in the service of self-control, peer interaction, conflict resolution, goal-attainment, problem solving, and mastery of the information world. The matrix of internal representations is increasingly complex, in mirror image of the more complex external world, and, one hopes, accompanied by the equally complex capacities to operate on those internal representations. Children learn roles and practice them internally and behaviorally, trying on new parts of their identity. They use internal images and selective attention to maintain goal-directed behavior in the face of frustration, or to delay gratification and control impulses.

According to most developmental theorists, the use of symbolic exchange to regulate behavior/activity is directly traced to early experiences in relationships. Representational capacity, language, metacognition, and problem solving, have all been linked to the quality of organization in early relationships (Greenberg et al., 1990). Like previous phases of adaptation, context plays a considerable role in the extent to which representational capacity is extended and organized within middle childhood, and is used in the service of competent adaptation to issues of self-control and identity. Availability of appropriate role models is one important feature of context—adult and older peer models play an increasingly important role in the regulation of children's behavior through middle childhood. Furthermore, learning tasks must also be available in ways that are linked to the ways in which the child has come to make meaning of the world—again in connection with role models, and in connection to real-world problem solving (Resnick, 1995).

The key developmental challenges described above are molar, global constructs. No single behavior will indicate competent or incompetent adaptation with respect to any challenge. Instead, quality of adaptation is indexed by patterns of behavior across situations that reflect these challenges. Furthermore, the quality of a child's adaptation in a certain situation is a function of (a) a developmental challenge that is appropriate for that phase, (b) the child's history of adaptation to previous developmental tasks, and (c) the affordance value provided by the context in that situation. If challenge is too great, if affordance value is low, or if developmental history indicates poor adaptation to challenges that underlie performance in that situation, then adaptation will be poor, no matter how competent the child was in previous themes. In this way risk extends across contexts (systems) and time.

The tasks described by developmental theorists are no more than names for ways in which systems are organized (Greenspan, 1989). Viewing child-context as a system, each developmental theme is basically a challenge to this system to reorganize itself into a more sophisticated form. The child-context system in infancy is a reflexive system with fairly rigid or fixed responses. The child-context system in the preschool period contains multiple means of interacting (behavior, symbols), with internal feedback loops (memory, beliefs, attributions, expectations) and decision-making capacity (Boulding, 1985). In the Contextual Systems Model development is marked not by changes within a particular domain (e.g., cognitive or motor development), but in the progress to more complex, sophisticated systems.

Developmental theorists view history as a primary explanation or "cause" (Sroufe, 1989), of current adaptation. In this perspective, the child brings his or her own developmental history to bear on any challenge, and for better or worse, success in meeting that demand will be determined in part by that history. This is a simple but fundamental truth that is not dealt with adequately in current views of education. Educators cannot hope to address adequately the needs of high-risk children without a thorough understanding of how their developmental history affects adaptation. Finally, the perspective strongly emphasizes that context plays a decisive role in what develops and how it develops.

In sum, any consideration of adaptation to developmental challenges in schooling contexts must identify those challenges (e.g., "readiness" or "preliteracy" or "time on task") in light of knowledge of (1) current adaptational capacity (complexity as a "system"), (2) history of prior adaptation, and (3) affordance value of school or classroom environment for children with respect to these challenges.

How Does Developmental History Affect Subsequent Adaptation?

With regard to education of young children this question is fundamental to the theoretical and practical underpinnings of the enterprise. Some might argue that by adopting a developmental perspective we are arguing that early development "fixes" the individual to a particular pathway or future. But according to Bowlby (1969), development is always the product of current circumstances and developmental history. For individuals interested in intervening, teaching, or otherwise affecting the course of development, the idea that previous development fixes future development would seem contrary to their endeavors and goals.

The Contextual Systems Model view of development, stated in the previous pages, is not at all in line with the idea that previous history fixes the future course or trajectory of children's adaptation or progress. The relation between developmental past, present, and future is strong; that is, developmental history plays a major role in the present and future, but the developing child is also an open system, so that current (or future) circumstances may interact with history to alter the course of development. The term "induction" refers to the extent to which current circumstances can alter or bring about the quality of adaptation shown by an individual. The distributed nature of adaptation is consistent with development as an open process.

Related to this issue of past and present is the concern about the degree to which development becomes increasingly "committed" to a certain outcome. Sroufe (1989) has used Waddington's model of a tree lying on its side to denote the idea that development proceeds along an ever-increasing number of branching pathways from a single starting point. Over time, the directions open to a pathway at a given nodal point become constrained by directions taken at earlier choice points, such that the number of possible final outcomes available become constrained as well. In this way, previous experience guides and constrains the available developmental outcomes.

School is a context in which development occurs. Therefore the process of schooling is a major influence on the pathways that development may take, regardless of the history of these paths. One theme made clear in Sroufe's (1989) notion of pathways is that across individuals (whose development can be modeled by the branching tree), a given outcome along the branching pathways can be traced back to any number of starting points, so that individuals may differ with respect to starting points, but based on history and experience, it is possible they may end up on common pathways. School plays a role, for better or worse, in defining pathways, in defining outcomes along pathways, and in creating common or divergent pathways along which children's development may proceed. Understanding the mechanisms by which schools operate in these regards is critical to a more comprehensive view of how schooling might affect the development of high-risk children.

Continuity in Development

We return to mechanisms by which the developmental past may affect the present and future. Many theorists identify the means by which the past affects the present and future. With development, previous forms of adaptation become layered, or nested, within present forms. For example, as the child moves from primary concerns of protection and safety (attachment) to exploration of the object world using the caregiver as a secure base from which to explore, the child's quality of adaptation to the attachment issue (e.g., secure, insecure) is organized within the emerging quality of adaptation to issues of exploration and how the parent will be used as a base for exploration. These relations between past and present create continuity in identity across time.

Thus the quality of the child's adaptation to exploration and mastery will build on the quality of adaptation to issues of attachment, and in turn adaptation to attachment challenges will be organized within the child's exploratory system. For the early elementary-school student, adaptation to challenges in peer relations and mastery of symbols (in literacy training or self-regulation) will be traceable to beliefs about self and others learned in relation to a caregiver, how emotion was regulated by the child-caregiver relationship, and the use of symbols to mediate experience in that relationship. A child-caregiver relationship in which the child learned to regulate emotion on his or her own, without the caregiver's assistance, where beliefs about self involved a sense of being unworthy, or where the meaning of symbols was distorted (I love you but I hit you), poses risks related to incompetent adaptation to school's challenges.

Aspects of adaptation to early challenges can be reactivated in the present under circumstances in which present situations make similar demands on the child, or that bear psychological resemblance to earlier issues, such as similarities between the early attachment relationship and the adolescent theme of connected emancipation. Patterns of interactive behavior between parent and child used to negotiate leave-taking (especially around situations with inherent

risk) are highly similar to those used by infant and caregiver to negotiate physical separations (Cassidy, 1994). In this way, past and present are connected by similarity in the challenges underlying
adaptation and the behavioral and relationship patterns used to
negotiate these themes.

Re-activation of Early Adaptation

Past and present are connected in another way, this time involving a
disjunction between current demands and previous history. On occasion situational challenges are too great for children, for example,
when a child lacking in any previous experience with peers is placed in
school in a classroom with 30 children and a teacher. Lacking previous
experience in such situations, "old" patterns of adaptation that worked
before may be reactivated, and the child may refuse to separate from
her parent, withdraw, or become highly passive and dependent as a
means of staying in close proximity to adult(s).

Similarly the child with an insecure attachment history (and associated lack of self-reliance) may be easily overwhelmed by the academic, problem-solving, and peer-relations challenges of elementary
school and use behaviors such as crying, hitting, and withdrawal as a
means of adapting to those challenges, when those behaviors are most
appropriately used by infants in relation to regulating arousal (Sroufe,
1989). Thus, previous patterns of adaptation can be re-activated in
present circumstances and may guide future adaptations for better or
worse, that is, the child will use whatever means is at her or his disposal to adapt. Some of these may mesh with the challenges of the situation, and some may not.

Attachment and School Adaptation

The relations between patterns of adaptation to the developmental
challenge of forming an effective attachment relationship with a primary caregiver, and adaptation to school are an example of how early
patterns of adaptation are carried forward into the school setting. The
literature is full of studies confirming the relation between infant
attachment status (secure, avoidant, ambivalent) and later developmental adaptation in preschool and school-age children (Erickson,
Sroufe, & Egeland, 1985; Greenberg et al., 1990; Sroufe, 1983; van
IZjendoorn & De Ruiter, 1993).

With respect to outcomes in the preschool years, attachment insecurity predicts a variety of problems, notably incompetence with
peers, overdependence on teachers, and lower self-confidence. In par-

ticular, children whose attachment to caregivers is classified as ambivalent demonstrate greater passivity or impulsiveness, whereas children with an avoidant stance toward their caregivers show more aggression and antisocial tendencies (Erickson et al., 1985; Sroufe, 1983). Sroufe and colleagues (summarized in Sroufe, 1989) have clearly demonstrated that children with insecure attachment histories explore more poorly, perform worse on tasks involving mastery and cognitive performance, and do more poorly on interactive tasks requiring the child to use an adult as a resource, than do children with secure attachment histories. Van IZjendoorn and De Ruiter (1993) summarize a line of research focusing on the learning and cognitive outcomes related to attachment, and convincingly demonstrate the linkages between attachment security and emergent literacy, peer relations, and problem solving in school situations. Furthermore, Pianta (1992) suggests that early relationship experiences around attachment issues lay the foundation for interaction with adults that influences subsequent adaptation in school contexts. Finally, Borkowski and Dukewich (in press) speculate that self-regulatory processes that emerge in the context of the attachment relationship, such as selective attention, the use of working memory, self-control, and interactions with adults, carry forward into cognitive and social tasks that children encounter in school.

Developmental history affects subsequent adaptation when the patterns of adaptation to previous challenges make subsequent adaptation to new challenges difficult or easy. Ample evidence shows that insecure child-parent attachments, especially avoidance, predict low levels of exploration, mastery, and peer competence in school (Sroufe, 1989). Here we have an example of the link between home interactions and school interactions. The process linking these patterns of adaptation is presumably the child's "learning" through repeated nonnurturing encounters with a caregiver to provide his own emotional reassurance and to acquire the belief that adults are not helpful and that he or she, the child, is not worthy of help. These are adaptive patterns (they make sense) when the caregiver is intrusive or punitive but these patterns are incompetent forms of adaptation when the "challenge" is to interact with a *helpful* adult (teacher). When this pattern of adaptation is "brought forward" in the dynamics of school, the capacity of the child-context system to flexibly self-regulate (i.e., signal for and accept adult resources as needed) is compromised and risk is present.

Similarly the child with an insecure attachment history may not be motivated to "move out" and explore the world in increasingly complex ways because the effectiveness of a caregiver (or teacher) as a secure base from which to explore is undermined in the case of insecure attachment. In a 1988 study by Bus and van IZjendoorn, children who were classified with avoidant attachments were far less competent in engaging in emergent literacy skills and activities than their peers with secure attachments.

These examples of the relations between attachment and adaptation to school and school-like situations demonstrate that patterns of adaptation to previous developmental issues (in this case, attachment) are latent, but available, in the child's efforts to adapt to current issues. That is, when a situation calls for a previous mode of adaptation, it becomes activated. Therefore, as the five-year-old is faced with increasingly complex demands for exploration and mastery (achievement), attachment issues may become activated, and the quality of the child's adaptation to attachment issues will become manifest. This child, in a kindergarten classroom with demands for mastery of print, may begin to look passive, angry, or inappropriately independent, or she may seek and use help from adults in a smooth and skillful manner. If the classroom demands increase, or if demands are not adapted to the child, her adaptational capacity becomes increasingly stressed, and less sophisticated levels of organization become activated, perhaps in the form of reflexive acting-out behavior.

For infants, preschoolers, and children in the primary grades (and later grades for many high-risk children), one cannot underestimate the extent to which relationships with people and environments support or inhibit developmental progress through the "challenges" noted previously. In a larger sense, the distributed nature of competence means that children are only as competent as their context affords them the opportunity to be. In short, their competence is a property of these systems—child and context. Context provides inputs to risk and to health.

The Contextual Systems Model view of development as regulated activity that becomes increasingly organized suggests that the early childhood period is one of heightened sensitivity to the influence of relationships, because of the prominence of relationships as regulators. Periods of heightened sensitivity to certain environmental stressors may occur. In the age range from two to five, children's development and competence are closely tied to the extent to which their context provides them with support for the developmental tasks of attachment, autonomy, mastery, communication, and self-control (Greenspan & Porges, 1984; Sroufe & Rutter, 1984). Environments that are structured, reciprocal, and sensitive to the child's cues, and that provide affectively positive stimulation support positive adaptation in the preschool years. For the preschooler, conditions that are most likely to have a strong impact are those altering the quality of affective stimulation available, those inducing changes or inconsistencies in contextual structure (e.g., rules), and those impacting the organization and structure of close relationships. Despite the myriad possible influences on children at this age, it is the way in which these influences are mediated by interpersonal and social relationships that primarily determines the salience of their impact.

SUMMARY

Children themselves are systems, developing in constant exchange with the contexts they contact. This perspective takes a long and wide view of risk. That is, risk that is seen in school has a long history; furthermore, it typically involves much more than what meets the eye. The risk apparent in a child's difficulty with reading most likely has connections with and roots in social and emotional processes. Likewise, contexts outside of the child will also be involved. It is the challenge to educators to understand how schools and schooling enters this developmental process and shapes it, for better or worse.

7

Life Hazards Contributing to Educational Risk

The present chapter aims to discuss the consequences for children's development of exposure to selected life hazards that directly or indirectly, affect the relationship between child/family and schooling. *Life hazards* are conditions that are known to undermine healthy development. They pose as considerable threats, or disturbances to developmental systems. As discussed by Sameroff (1989), developmental systems as depicted in the Contextual Systems Model are challenged by a wide range of factors, many of which are simply minor perturbations that can be easily responded to by the self-regulatory properties of the system. On the other hand, a wide range of factors pose greater challenges to a developmental system, requiring significant reorganization of the system in order for the system to reach a point of adaptation or "fit" with the challenge. Life hazards are those challenges that require reorganization that undermines the capacity of the system to support adequate development.

Many readers will be familiar with the literature described in this chapter as studies of "life stress" or "stressors" (Pianta, Egeland, & Sroufe, 1990). The term "life hazard" is used for a number of reasons. First, the use of "life" in life hazard suggests a long view of its effects; the term indicates that exposure may have long-term consequences, not only consequences in terms of directly altering a trajectory toward a particular outcome (as in the case of teratogen exposure and cognitive development) but, more importantly, less direct consequences that will be intertwined and dependent on subsequent conditions and experiences. Second, the use of "hazard" indicates that exposure to the condition or event under consideration is largely out of the child's control, and under most circumstances, exposure is something to be avoided. In this chapter, life hazards describe a range of events and conditions that carry with them the potential to divert developmental trajectories toward negative outcomes, or to reduce the likelihood of attaining positive outcomes.

POVERTY AND SOCIAL CLASS

Mickey Kaus (1992) has argued that an increasingly problematic contemporary reality is that money has never meant more than it does today, that money (social class), dictates social interaction in a way that it never has previously. The leveling mechanisms of previous generations, for example, the military draft, which forced people to come together across social classes, have disappeared. Kaus talks of the disappearance of "public spheres," places where people congregated regularly regardless of class: the downtown square on a Saturday morning, or public parks, for example.

Christopher Jencks (1988) pointed out that "in 1985 the Census Bureau released data showing that poor urban families were more likely to have poor neighbors in 1980 than 1970.... The main cause was increased residential segregation along economic lines. This change was especially marked for blacks. No one knows for sure whether this trend has continued since 1980. But...most observers assume [it has]" (p. 30).

Two points need to be emphasized. First, public schools can become Kaus' "public spheres," something they no longer are in much of the country, particularly in large cities, where public schools are largely attended by the poor and minorities. Second, in a society where money becomes increasingly important in defining who one is in that society, not having money intensifies risk in a way that it did not heretofore. Intensification of this sort suggests that hazards such as poverty, poor housing, and poor schools operate in an organized, systemic manner.

SYSTEMS OF LIFE HAZARDS

Life hazards are *organized* in systems. Although most of the discourse on life hazards (poverty, divorce, malnutrition) focuses on these hazards singly, it is a fact that hazards are interrelated to an exceptionally high degree in many instances. Using Super and Harkness' (1986) concept of the developmental niche as reflecting the organization of influences external to the child on development (culture, etc.), it is accurate to say that "risk" often reflects development in hazardous niches. Attention to the niche-like nature, or systemic features of life hazards, is critical for understanding the ways in which these systems can be broken up. For example, Garbarino (1982) points out that in Western European countries, poverty is nowhere near as highly associated with poor child outcomes as it is in the United States. The reason for this, according to Garbarino, is that the links between poverty and other life hazards (child maltreatment, for example) have been broken by systematic application of social-intervention programs or societal structures compensating for poverty. The systemic nature of life hazards greatly increases their threat to the child/family system. This system can respond to challenges reflected by single hazards, but can be quickly exhausted or can fail to adapt, as linked hazards continue to present challenges. Attention to the interrelated nature of life hazards and appreciation of their existence as systems can yield interventions with the potential to alter risk coefficients.

The interrelated, organized nature of life hazards is frequently omitted in discussions of stress in early childhood. The literature most frequently talks about the effects of a particular life hazard (e.g., divorce, parental psychiatric problems) without attention to how these hazards are nested with other hazards within "niches." Even more importantly this literature is translated into practice, so that children exposed to one of these "risk factors" are placed in an intervention that may not address the range of associated life hazards, or worse yet, are labeled and routed into alternative programs that end up delaying their exposure to the curriculum that their unlabeled peers experience (Walsh et al., 1992). Intervention eligibility, when driven by a single, linear cause, is likely to obscure, rather then meet, the needs of the child.

In the real world, exposure to one hazard (e.g., parental divorce or poverty) entails exposure to a constellation, or system, of hazards, which, as a group, frequently have an impact above and beyond the sum of their individual impacts (Rutter, 1979). Rutter demonstrated that as exposure to hazards increased in linear fashion (summed), the behavior problems associated with hazard exposure increased geometrically (multiplied). Thus the "whole" of hazard exposure was greater than the sum of the parts. In a study predicting IQ (intelligence quotient) in economically disadvantaged families, Sameroff et al. (1987) demonstrated that of ten hazards investigated, it was the number of hazards to which children were exposed (e.g., parental psychopathology, inadequate nutrition), not the type of hazard, that accounted for the largest proportion of variance in IQ at age four. Moreover, as the number of hazards increased, there was a concomitant decrease in IQ at each age between four and thirteen (Sameroff, Seifer, Baldwin, & Baldwin, 1993).

Schorr and Schorr (1988) argued that risk factors interact, causing their effects to multiply. The child already having problems due to low birth weight, prenatal exposure to alcohol or drugs, or poor nutrition is at the same time especially vulnerable to a damaging home environment. A child who must adapt to a home environment that includes being unwanted, being part of an overly large family, or abuse by a highly stressed parent is especially vulnerable to the damaging effects of a school that expects little and provides little. Schorr also points out that if risks multiply one another, then interventions that reduce one risk factor can have relatively large effects by removing a multiplier. Again, systems models are necessary for comprehending the nature of interventions that can respond to hazardous systems.

The Dynamic of Hazard Exposure and Resource Availability

Life hazards can also act as agents of developmental change to the extent that they provide challenges for adaptation to the family, school, or child. Mild hazards, or hazards to systems in which there is a high concentration of resources for development, can act as perturbations (Sameroff & Emde, 1989) that induce normative, healthy self-stabilizing and self-reorganizing forces in the child and family system that strengthen the capacity of these systems to respond to other challenges in the future. Events such as changing schools or jobs have been shown under some circumstances to induce positive changes in a family system.

To the extent that sufficient resources exist within the family and child (and other) systems, there is evidence that certain hazards are not pathogenic for the child or family, and that after a period of reorganization, healthy functioning is possible and frequently occurs (see Hetherington [1989] for a discussion of the divorce literature). Identifying the balance between hazards and resources in family, school, and child systems that distinguishes between healthy and problem development is difficult, and the first step is appreciation of the systemic nature of the problem.

Healthy Development and Hazard Exposure

Suggesting that positive consequences may follow hazard exposure should not obscure several central facts. First, young children have very few of the coping skills and resources necessary for buffering themselves from the impact of life hazards; moreover, the systemic nature of life hazards usually results in double and triple exposure for children. On their own, children are powerless to alter their exposure to hazards such as divorce, poverty, or maltreatment. Nor are they capable of unlinking one hazard from an associated hazard. Other systems (parents, other adults, communities, schools) are responsible for regulating the exposure of children to life hazards, and for providing the resources to balance the effects of hazard exposure. Children who develop apparently unscathed by hazard exposure do not come by this healthy state on their own (Werner & Smith, 1982).

Also important, the literature on positive consequences of hazard exposure often focuses on single exposures to mild hazards in systems in which resources for development are relatively plentiful (e.g., changing schools once while living in a middle-class household and neighborhood). Hazard exposure under these circumstances should not be equated with exposure to the same hazard under other circumstances (changing schools five times in the first two years while living with a single mother in dangerous neighborhoods). Many children are exposed to multiple severe hazards in systems where there are few resources.

Young children are dependent on parents, family members, communities, and schools, that is, upon a system, for resources related to balancing the effects of life hazards. A comprehensive analysis suggests that viewing hazards as opportunities for growth and development is often a semantic twist to what is otherwise an experience that produces a negative trend in development that can be predicted with great regularity. No amount of semantic change or identification of individual success stories can mask the overwhelming evidence that for the population of children as a whole, life hazards are to be avoided, and it is the responsibility of the adult population to respond to this need. Renaming the consequences of hazard exposure (i.e., calling "at risk" "at promise") or finding kids that somehow made it through life hazards (resilient children) can do more to obscure the immediacy of the need than to inform the discourse on meeting that need. We find that the primary contribution of the literature on healthy development in children exposed to life hazards is that it calls attention to features of the developmental system responding to hazard exposure.

LIFE HAZARDS FOR YOUNG CHILDREN AND THEIR IMPACT ON SCHOOL ADJUSTMENT

Research Issues

Rutter (1987) suggests that an understanding of the impact of life hazards can only be gained by an examination of the individual and systemic response to the hazard, emphasizing the interactive processes involved. The great majority of research and conceptual work in the field of stress and children, however, considers the effects of hazards from a "main effects" position. There is assumed to be a direct impact of a hazard that is reflected in the correlation between exposure and some child outcome or in the difference in outcomes associated with exposure and nonexposure.

This research base has led to a naive and simplistic perspective that (1) hazard exposure can be reduced to exposure to a single event (not a system of interrelated problems), (2) the impact of hazards on development can be understood in isolation from the systems in which exposure takes place (child, peer, family), and (3) the pernicious effects of hazard exposure can be eliminated by culling exposed children into intervention programs targeted at the effects of a single risk factor. For example, the impact of an intervention for children exposed to poverty is different for the child for whom this may be the only serious hazard to which he or she is exposed, than for the child for whom this is only one of many hazards (Ramey & Campbell, 1991).

This section reviews the empirical evidence for the relation between certain life hazards and the development of young children. Of particular interest is the contribution to problems in the relationship between the child/family system and schooling. Following Sameroff's (1989) discussion on regulatory codes in different levels of the social environment, this discussion is organized around hazards present in communities, subcultures, and neighborhoods, and relationship-based hazards present in small social groups of family and peer relations. The studies that follow are largely descriptive, and they vary widely in methodological sophistication.

Cultural, Community, Family Hazards

Poverty

Public health statistics on young children in poverty highlight their need and were cited in chapter 1. The picture they paint is not positive with respect to any aspect of development. Children reared in poverty tend to have lower birth weights, an increased probability of death due to disease, increased susceptibility to disease agents, poor prenatal care, decreased gestational spacing, and younger mothers. Poverty is associated with elevated incidence for a variety of negative outcomes for children including death, homelessness, burns, injuries, emergency room visits, lack of adequate health care, having a disability, infectious disease, vision and hearing problems, childhood AIDS (aquired immunodeficiency syndrome), and maltreatment, to name several.

Children who grow up in poor families are less likely to show secure attachments to their caretakers in infancy than children from middle- and upper-class homes (van IZjendoorn, Goldberg, Kroonenberg, & Frenkel, 1992). They are more likely to be rated by their parents as exhibiting difficult temperaments, and they show a wide range of behavior problems that are more severe than for middle-class children—problems such as depression, peer conflict, and conduct problems (e.g., Tonge, James, & Hillam, 1975; see also chapter 1, this volume).

Several descriptions of children living in poverty, with the often associated culture of violence, demonstrate that these children are under extreme psychological distress. They often show symptoms of Post Traumatic Stress Disorder, including flashbacks, an inability to focus attention due to mental distractions, lack of motivation, apathy and depression, and unpredictable behaviors (Garbarino et al., 1992). In fact, Garbarino describes children living in our large cities as living in "war zones": "A study conducted in one of Chicago's public housing projects revealed that the No. 1 fear parents have for their young children is being shot" (Garbarino et al., 1992, p. 6). The psychological and emotional distress associated with living under dangerous, stressful, unpredictable conditions are some of the primary reasons why these children have difficulty attending and learning in classroom settings (Garbarino et al., 1992). Yet if these children are diagnosed with Attention Deficit Hyperactivity Disorder, or Learning Disability, what sense does it make to locate "disorder" within them or within their culture? How disruptive to their schooling is it to define them as disordered when the systems surrounding the relation between their experience in and out of school is so unregulated?

Poverty stresses caretakers and households in ways that have a direct impact on children's development (McLoyd & Wilson, 1991). Adults who are poor or who have sustained recent economic losses are more vulnerable to a wide range of mental health problems. Although research indicates that parents in poverty are exposed to a large number of additional life hazards as a consequence of poverty, there are also findings indicating that these individuals also respond less adaptively to hazards as a function of cumulative hazard exposure. That is, because of the fact that so many other life hazards are associated with poverty, poverty status induces a generalized decline in adaptive capacity (Pianta & Egeland, 1995). Poor mothers are more likely to be depressed, and parents of low income and poor families tend to exhibit a more restrictive, punitive caretaking style and perceive the child as a stressful burden on their already taxed capacities (McLoyd & Wilson, 1991).

The niche-like influence of poverty is evident in the United States in terms of the number of hazards associated with poverty. For example, low income is associated with child abuse and neglect, social deprivation and general environmental inadequacy, maternal unresponsivity and passivity, and characteristics in the child of negative mood, greater intensity, clinginess, lower cognitive functioning, and higher scores on behavior problem scales (e.g., McLoyd & Wilson, 1991). Several authors conclude that poverty and ethnicity in the United States combine to form a population that has much more similarity to Third World nations than it does to the remainder of the U.S. population (see, for example, David Rieff's 1991 book, *Los Angeles: Capitol of the Third World.*

In a classic study of children reared in poverty in the United Kingdom, Tonge et al. (1975) described a disorder of lifestyle characterized by insularity, economic hardship, low social organization, adults who are marginally depressed and maladjusted, and children who, at the least, suffer from material deprivation, neglect, and lack of supervision. Mothers in these families were depressed, and fathers were seen as impulsive and prone to aggression. Children had a higher mortality rate than the general population, more discipline problems, and poor skills. Importantly, exceptions to these patterns of development appeared to be a function of the children having positive school experiences.

It is quite possible that much work on children and families in poverty has not been as culturally informed and sensitive as it should be. But to dismiss the realities of poverty is to fall into a naive romanticism under the guise of cultural sensitivity. Poverty is hard on people, and it is getting harder all the time.

Many investigators have noted that the link between poverty and negative child outcomes is not universal across societies or constant across time. This is in large part because the effects of poverty on children are mediated by the hazards associated with poverty. These mediating factors include housing, nutrition, health care, child care, schooling, parental stress, accumulating hazards, and developmental problems in the child (Huston, 1991). Consequently, breaking the link between low income and these associated hazards can be a major preventive influence.

Consider the metaphor of the Third World country within the developed United States. It is very clear that poverty prescribes a set of living conditions best understood as a developmental niche, each condition within the niche associated with negative consequences for children, and the very existence of these conditions as a niche within our society predicts negative consequences for the society as a whole. When all the various systems and subsystems related to schooling-child/family relationship are affected by poverty, it is nearly impossible to think the child within these systems will function competently in school.

Social Insularity

Social contact extending outside of a household is a critical factor in the development of a child. Caregivers' relationships with persons outside the home are an important source of support and help. Moreover these contacts frequently generate opportunities for peer contact for the children involved. The absence of these forms of social contact has been identified as a detriment to development.

Engaging in and maintaining nurturing and supportive social contacts has been linked to numerous positive outcomes for children (Crnic, Greenberg, Ragozin, Robinson, & Basham 1980; Crockenberg, 1981). Garbarino (1982) defines support as connections that occur whenever individuals (e.g., parents, teachers) or systems (schools, churches, families) have ongoing contact with each other that is organized around concern for the welfare of the child. One value of social support for caregivers or individuals exposed to life hazards appears to be in its provision of psychological or emotional resources. In addition, obtaining transportation, needed food, clothing, or child careis of tremendous value in shielding many caregivers, and in turn their children, from the negative impact of hazards (Belle, 1982).

Coercive parenting and child aggression appear to be related directly to mothers' insularity. Lack of social support has been associated with child abuse and marital violence (Strauss, Gelles, & Steinmetz, 1980). Conversely, parent-training techniques intended to reduce coercion and aggression are most effective on days when mothers have positive social contacts outside of the intervention experience (Wahler, Leske, & Rogers, 1979).

Pianta and Ball (1993) examined the effect of social contact of mothers on children's schooling. For parents of children entering kindergarten, the number of supportive contacts reported by mothers was a significant predictor of quality of mother-child interaction and teachers' reports of children's behavioral adjustment to kindergarten (Ball & Pianta, 1993; Pianta & Ball, 1993), an effect that was intensified in the highest risk groups.

That social contacts are important should not surprise anyone, given the inherently social nature of human beings. Human systems are social in nature. People who are denied supportive social contacts are being denied something that is very necessary to humans.

Unemployment

Parental, especially paternal, unemployment is a visible and potent hazard for families and children, in large part because it threatens poverty with its associated hazards. As Judith Jones noted, "Children are not poor, they have poor parents" (1994, p. 2).

With an annual incidence rate estimated at nearly 20% of the male work force, and with most of these being younger, less-experienced workers who tended to have children, nearly ten million children annually experienced some form of paternal unemployment in the early 1980s (Margolis, 1982). These children are the cohort on which have been based many of the reports documenting failure in the public schools. The Children's Defense Fund estimates that in 1990 alone, 2.8 million families with children had an unemployed family member. Considering the rate of underemployment and unreported unemployment, any estimate of child exposure to parental unemployment is most likely low.

The linking of unemployment to other life hazards (notably poverty) translates into unemployment being a potentially more potent hazard. In recent years unemployment occurred with much greater frequency among younger, less-skilled, less-educated, black workers. Unemployment rose dramatically for young blacks in the 1970s and 1980s (Jencks, 1988). In 1989 unemployment was associated with homelessness for children and parents (Masten, 1992).

In terms of its more direct effects on children, paternal unemployment has been associated with child abuse (e.g., Garbarino et al., 1992), family violence (Strauss et al., 1980), depression, and psychiatric disturbance (Huston, 1991). Unemployment is also implicated in intergenerational cycles of poverty, poor education, and poor work skills. Interestingly, raising children is viewed as a major hazard by women who are themselves unemployed and desirous of work (Canam, 1986). In a recent study of 236 single African-American mothers, unemployment predicted maternal depression, negative perceptions about motherhood, and maternal punitiveness. Children's perceptions of family financial problems and their relationship with their mothers were predictive of a variety of behavioral and emotional problems (McLoyd, Javartne, Ceballo, & Borquez, 1994).

As has been emphasized repeatedly throughout this book, linkages among life hazards, or the systemic nature of risk, raise considerable challenges to educators and social policymakers. The example of unemployment is one such case in which events distal from the child's school experience can have a profound impact on schooling.

Household Organization and Stimulation

One hazard often overlooked in most considerations of risk, but that has a strong impact on children's development, is the degree of organization and structure available in a household. Household organization is directly linked to the extent to which the child receives developmentally appropriate stimulation for learning and cognitive development—the affordance value of the environment. Bradley and colleagues (1988) have researched this area for the past 15 years and identified characteristics of the home environment that underlie cognitive development and predict a range of school outcomes.

In the 1970s, using the Home Observation for the Measurement of the Environment (HOME), Caldwell and Bradley (e.g., Bradley & Caldwell, 1976) found that facets of the household in which a child lives, such as maternal responsivity and involvement (e.g., reading to a child, talking to the child during the home visit), household organization (e.g., regular schedules of feeding, waking, and other routines), and provision of appropriate play materials (e.g., whether toys are available in the home and accessible to the child) were predictive of cognitive development across the preschool years and well into the primary grades. More important, changes in ratings on these scales correlated with improvements and decrements in intellectual test scores across the same developmental period.

In a follow-up study, Bradley et al. (1988) analyzed the longitudinal effects of the preschool home environment on academic and behavioral adjustment in school. Their findings indicate that parental responsivity measured as early as infancy predicted classroom behavior in elementary school. Other aspects such as parental involvement in school, provision of play materials, and support for learning acted to maintain cognitive growth. These analyses indicate an interaction among phases of development, aspects of the home environment, and outcomes in school. Conversely studies of home environment indicate deleterious effects on cognitive test scores for overcrowding, unwanted stimulation (noise), random changes in activities, and unpredictability (cf. Wachs, 1992).

Neighborhood Hazards

Although professionals who work with children readily acknowledge that living in a particular neighborhood can affect a young child, there has been little empirical work on this important influence on children. Recent attention to neighborhood-level effects indicate that neighborhoods exert a moderating influence on life hazards such as poverty and violence (Entwistle & Alexander, 1993).

Garbarino and Sherman (1980) were among the first to document the effects on child development of a neighborhood. In their study, neighborhoods of equivalent socioeconomic status were examined for rates of child maltreatment, and interviews with residents established what factors were associated with differential rates of maltreatment. The comparisons revealed the importance of informal support networks within these neighborhoods. "Safe" and "dangerous" neighborhoods were readily identified by postal carriers, as well as children and adult residents. The "safe" neighborhoods had reduced rates of child abuse, were those in which more neighborhood services were available (e.g., a recreational center), and in which caregivers had regular contact with one another and could count on others to provide them with help in the form of transportation or child care. Importantly, these networks were apparent to visitors and residents despite the equivalent poverty of the neighborhoods.

Neighborhood-level indicators appear to have greater influence for boys than for girls of similar risk status. During the first two years of school, boys engage in more activities outside of the home and in neighborhoods than girls, and gains in mathematics achievement during this period appear linked to outside-the-home activities for boys more than for girls (Entwistle & Alexander, 1993). Moreover, boys experience more violence and aggression outside of the home in the neighborhood than do girls, and staying in school appears linked to peer and other influences that occur in the context of the neighborhood (Duncan, 1993; Spencer, 1993).

Finally, Garbarino's (Garbarino et al., 1992) summary of life in inner-city Chicago housing projects suggests that neighborhood violence and war-zone environments create a context for the development of traumatic reactions and psychological distress. Distress and trauma to the child related to incidents of violence but had greatest negative impact when accumulated within a larger environment of violence and urban decay.

Relationship Hazards

In keeping with Sameroff's (1989) scheme for organizing levels of the social environment, we turn to a discussion of life hazards located in closer proximity to the child: in relationship systems within the home.

Marital Relationships and Single Parenting

Belsky (1984) claimed that the marital relationship serves as the principal support system for parents in their development of caregiving skills. Overt discord, violence, or lack of support between spouses or partners can be serious hazards for young children. Low support or emotional tension in the marital dyad is associated with less affectionate and sensitive, more punitive and restrictive parental styles (Crnic et al., 1983). Spousal violence is associated with authoritarian and restrictive parenting styles and child abuse within the immediate family (Strauss et al., 1980). Recent work indicates that witnessing discord and negative interactions between parents raises children's anxiety and insecurity to the extent that it impairs performance on cognitive and problem-solving tasks (Hennesy, Rabideau, Cicchetti, & Cummings, 1994). Exposure to discord and violence between adults in the home has been implicated in developmental models of serious conduct problems.

Although marital discord is definitely a life hazard with considerable consequences, divorce and separation are events requiring considerable reorganization within the family and child systems. Almost all children experience divorce and separation as painful and show some type of short-term effects; the long-term effects of divorce have been debated but recent evidence suggests some lasting effects for both boys and girls (Hetherington, 1989; McLanahan, Astone, & Marks, 1991; Whitehead, 1993). Short-term effects include lowered self-esteem, anger toward the custodial and noncustodial parent, decreased school adjustment and achievement, self-deprecation and blame, increased dependency on teachers and custodial parents, and increased depressive mood and acting out behavior (e.g., Emery,

1982; Hetherington, 1989; Pianta, Egeland, & Hyatt, 1986).

Whereas the short-term consequences of divorce are primarily the product of the marital separation, the long-term consequences are a function of the quality of postdivorce relations between the parents and with their children (Hetherington, 1989), as well as the child's resolution of the relationship disruption or loss experience. Negative long-term consequences include lower occupational and academic attainment, elevated prevalence of depression, anxiety and other psychiatric symptoms, and higher rates of relationship disruption (Hetherington, 1989). Divorce brings sudden, and often lasting, income loss to women and children (Duncan, 1991).

Jencks (1988) describes the effects of cultural norms about marriage and divorce on childrens' health and development, especially as these are mediated by social class. Some groups are particularly vulnerable to exposure to parental divorce and separation and its attendant negative influences. Jencks (1988) reports that in 1985 fewer than 40% of black children were born to a mother living with a husband—less than 25% in some large cities. "Some of these unwed mothers eventually marry, but since most black marriages end in divorce, a black child's chances of growing up in an intact family are extremely low" (p. 27).

> For less-privileged couples, however, the demise of traditional norms about marriage and divorce pose more serious problems. Once poor couples' relatives began to accept marital breakups as normal, their divorce rate soared. Divorce is far costlier for women with limited schooling and job skills than for upper-middle-class women. Poorly educated ex-husbands can seldom afford to support two households, and they seldom make adequate child-support payments. Nor are these women in a strong competitive position if they want to remarry. Poor children have suffered the most from our newly permissive approach to reproduction. Shotgun weddings and lifetime marriages caused adults a lot of misery, but they ensured that almost every child had a claim on some adult male's earnings. That is no longer the case. (Jencks, 1988, pp. 29–30)

Although divorce in some families is perceived with relief and hope for positive change, it nevertheless is a challenge requiring extensive reorganization. Divorce can precipitate the hazards of raising a child in a single-parent family, downward drift in terms of occupational and social status, decreased social support and income, parenting a child dealing with parental loss, and battles over custody and visitation. Children of divorced parents are less likely to have financial support for college (Whitehead, 1993), a serious issue when one considers that the cost of college rose 32% (in constant dollars) from 1980 to 1991 (U.S. Department of Education, 1993). Furthermore, these potential outcomes of divorce have been associated with greater home disorganization, diminished quality and quantity of adult attention and caretaking, lack of role models, and custodial parent experiences of anxiety, helplessness, depression, and family discord (e.g., Hetherington, 1989).

Finally, there is evidence that the impact of divorce on developmental trajectories is greater with younger children, especially in the preschool period. Children at this age appear especially vulnerable to discord and relationship disruption, perhaps due to their emergent social cognition, perspective-taking, and self-system development at the same time as they remain highly dependent on the family system and parent-child relationship systems. Their newly emerging skills and awareness in the social and self-development arenas are a fragile growth area in the hierarchy of developmental skills. The organization and trajectory of this process is highly open to input from relationship and family contexts during early childhood. When critical regulatory systems (family system, parent-child relationship, marital relationship) become a source of threat or hazard or are less available, there are negative effects on the child's own developmental skills in social and self-development (Sroufe & Fleeson, 1986).

The conditions associated with raising a child alone, one product of separation or divorce, put significant strain on personal, financial, and emotional resources, especially when they occur during the years in which the child is most needful of direct, involved, responsive caregiving (Belle, 1982; McLanahan et al., 1991). The hazards of single parenthood become even worse when combined with poverty or insularity (McLoyd & Wilson, 1991). Hetherington (1989), summarizing the literature on divorce, notes that middle-class, single parents who were recently divorced found child care particularly taxing and stressful, especially with their sons, and tended to be more angry, restrictive, punitive, and less structured in household operations than parents who acted as controls. For poor parents, single parenting is associated with poor child outcomes, but this association sometimes disappears after controlling for income (Munroe, Boyle, & Offord, 1988). Weissman, Leaf, and Bruse (1987) note that many of the differences seen in various studies between single and married mothers on psychological and social functioning variables are related to large financial differences between them.

Disrupted and/or single parenting is a hazard to which a very large proportion of children are exposed. Although associated with drops in income and made more hazardous when combined with poverty, single parenting is highly prevalent across income strata. In 1985 the proportion of children living in female-headed households was 21%, and if present trends continue, more than half (perhaps as high as 60%) of the children born in the 1980s will live in a single-parent household some time before they reach the age of 18. Importantly, children from single-parent households (disrupted or never-married) are less likely to complete high school and have low earnings as adults (McLanahan et al., 1991).

Clearly, divorce, separation, and martial discord affect the relationship between child/family and schooling systems. These life hazards directly and indirectly alter a substantial proportion of the resources for development present within these systems and challenge subsequent efforts to improve resources. Perhaps Bronfenbrenner (1986) captured the essence of this literature best when he said that it is best for a child to develop under conditions in which someone is in love with them, and even better when there are two people.

Child Maltreatment

Being maltreated by parents is a life hazard embedded in the parent-child relationship, exposure to which raises a child's risk for a number of problem outcomes related to social, emotional, and school adjustment (Cicchetti, 1994). Although traditionally attention has been focused on acts of physical or sexual abuse, for many children there are other maltreatment experiences. Most researchers recognize at least four forms of maltreatment: physical abuse, sexual abuse, physical neglect, and emotional neglect. Common across each form of maltreatment is a negative psychological effect (Garbarino & Vondra, 1987). In fact, Garbarino and Vondra (1987) suggest the term "psychological maltreatment" as a construct describing the psychological effects of all forms of maltreatment. The following section describes a unique set of studies on the effects on parental maltreatment of children. This program of research very clearly depicts systems in action, and their effect on developmental trajectories as children enter the early school years.

The Mother-Child Research Project at the University of Minnesota has tracked the development of a sample of 200 poor children from their birth onward. Using the project data base, Erickson, Egeland, and Pianta (1989) traced the consequences of four different forms of maltreatment (physical abuse, neglect, psychological unavailability, and sexual abuse) from birth through the first grade. Thirty-three (16.5%) children were classified as maltreated at 1 year, 44 (22%) at 2 years, and 47 (23.5%) at 6 years of age, indicating the high degree of overlap between poverty and child maltreatment. Furthermore, there was considerable overlap among the forms of maltreatment—more than half of the children experienced two or more forms of maltreatment.

Maltreatment was very stable. Across the six-year span of the this particular study, nearly two-thirds of the children who had ever been maltreated continued to be maltreated more than three years later. In most cases, stability in maltreatment was linked to stability in the numerous other factors that predicted maltreatment (e.g., poverty, depression, substance abuse).

In the Minnesota study, physically abused children and children exposed to psychologically unavailable parenting functioned poorly on a variety of assessments. At 18 months they were highly overrepresented among anxiously attached children, and at 24 months they were angry and noncompliant when interacting with their mothers, and showed declining scores on ability tests. In a problem-solving situation with their mothers at 42 months they showed noncompliance, low self-esteem, and poor self-control, were less effective problem solvers, and did not use their mother as an effective resource. In preschool settings these children remained negative, angry, noncompliant, overdependent, and hostile toward peers. They were rated by their kindergarten and first-grade teachers as aggressive and noncompliant, and had poor peer relations and problems with attention and academic achievement in the classroom. Approximately 50% of these children were referred for special education by the end of the first grade.

Neglected children were the least competent in school. These children were exposed to chronic lack of material resources, and their caregiving environments were unhealthy, unsafe, and lacking in supervision or stimulation. These children displayed many aspects of maladaptation throughout infancy and early childhood, similar to those described above for physical abuse and psychologically unavailable care. In kindergarten and first grade, however, the neglected children were profoundly maladjusted. They were rejected and unpopular, showing a mixture of aggression and withdrawal; they lacked the social skills necessary to engage peers competently. Toward teachers they responded with a similar lack of skill, displaying a marked maladaptation to academic and preacademic tasks. They lacked persistence, attentiveness, or motivation, often wandering aimlessly around the room. A striking proportion—80%—of these children were referred for special education by the end of first grade.

Erickson and colleagues (1989) also studied 11 children who had been sexually abused. These children tended to come from homes in which the mother was highly stressed, often by a violent male partner. Adult supervision was low, and the ability of the mothers of this group of children to protect their children was questionable. The sexually abused children showed marked extremes in behavior in school. Individually teachers described them as fluctuating from extreme aggression to marked passivity and dependence. Nearly all were characterized by extreme anxiety and marked dependence on adults. They all performed poorly on academic tasks, and half were referred for special education by the end of first grade.

The Minnesota study is representative of the majority of findings on the consequences of maltreatment. A number of equally sophisticated and detailed longitudinal studies confirm the conclusion that the many forms of child maltreatment often overlap, remain stable across several years, and have deleterious consequences for children's development in every conceivable area that would effect their adjustment in school. These studies indicate the pervasive effects of maltreatment on the child as a developing system. No domain of development appears left untouched by this experience: motor, language, social, cognitive, and emotional development are affected (Beeghly & Cicchetti, 1994; Cummings, Hennesy, Rabideau, & Cicchetti, 1994; Dodge, Pettit, & Bates, 1994; Erickson et al., 1989). Aber and Allen (1987) call the effects a fundamental risk to the child's "secure readiness to learn" (p. 410).

This discussion of the effects of maltreatment on development calls attention to the fact that many times a "disorder" that is located within the child by certain eligibility or classification mechanisms (e.g., special-education placement), has essentially been manufactured by the child-rearing system. However, it is critical to emphasize that child maltreatment occurs in a system of influences (cultures, neighborhoods, communities) and is not the sole responsibility of mothers (or fathers). Interestingly, the rates of child maltreatment noted above far exceed those for other western democracies, largely because the influences of culture and community on the family unit manages to disrupt the effects of other influences (e.g., poverty) on child rearing.

Parental Psychiatric Distress

Recently, considerable attention has been paid to the effects of maternal depression on child rearing and children. A large group of studies indicate maternal depression is associated with child maladjustment in the preschool years. Children of depressed mothers show elevated prevalence of insecure attachments to parents (DeMulder & Radke-Yarrow, 1991; Lyons-Ruth, 1992), less competent play behaviors, and greater problem behaviors than children of nondepressed mothers (Rubin, Both, Zahn-Waxler, Cummings, & Wilkinson, 1991), and a variety of problems in school adjustment, including lower academic achievement, poor social skills, and increased likelihood for referral to special education.

The social and behavioral problems of children of depressed mothers have roots as early as the 3–6-month period, during which it has been shown with great regularity that infants respond with distress and avoidance to mothers' depressed behaviors during interaction (Field, 1989). The patterns of self-regulation that the infant must develop in order to adapt to an emotionally unavailable or inconsistent parent are thought to be the precursors to later problems in emotional and social behavior. These effects during early infancy appear to account for the greater prevalence of insecure attachments assessed in the second year of life and onward (Cohn, Campbell, Matias, & Hopkins, 1990).

Peer Rejection

Although many of the life hazards discussed previously are the product of, or mediated by, the parent-child relationship, it is important also to recognize the role of peers in the child/family-schooling relationship. There is no question that previous hazard exposure (e.g., child maltreatment) makes peer relations problematic for many children, and in turn peer problems themselves become new hazards in these children's lives. This is a clear example of the kind of linking or chaining of hazards that occurs for many children, in which the sequelae of exposure to one hazard creates secondary hazards. For this reason, the transition to peer contexts may be a critical juncture for intervention aimed at unlinking this chain and establishing a new trajectory of development (Reid, 1994).

Without intervention, incompetence in peer relations is a highly stable factor in children's lives as early as the preschool years and can predict many negative future outcomes (Ladd, Price, & Hart, 1988). Problems with peers in preschool settings predict subsequent problems in school with considerable regularity (Ladd et al., 1988; Parker & Asher, 1987). Rejection by peers and aggression with peers appear to be uniquely hazardous conditions for children; rejection marks their exclusion from the benefits of peer contact, and aggression marks emergent antisocial characteristics (Parker & Asher, 1987). Peer rejection, as distinguished from neglect by peers, is predicted by a number of poor parenting practices and lack of skills in social cognition, perspective-taking, and self-control (Dodge et al., 1994). Its consequences for the child include grade retention, dropping out of school, underachievement, and delinquency.

Conversely, when adults intervene to guide, but not direct, young children's peer relations, chances are greater that these children will form better relations in the future (Reid, 1994). Sroufe's (1983) study of the preschool adjustment of maltreated children strongly supports the conclusion that there will be continuity in the types of relations formed by stressed children between parents and peers. Sroufe also suggests, however, that new relationships with teachers and well-adjusted peers can begin to counteract some of these earlier models of the self and the world, which may improve the child's adjustment.

SUMMARY

As has been discussed, many systems exert regulatory influence on children's development. Hazards that arise within these relationship systems all elevate risk for problems in school or for development of skills necessary for successful school adjustment. This review points out (1) the interrelated nature of life hazards, (2) the organized, systemic nature of risk, and (3) the persistence of risk over time and consequences for developmental decline. Together, these points indicate that indeed, many of the problems that children present in school, from lack of readiness to behavior problems, are not at all located in their heads, their families, or their schools. Instead, childrens' "pathologies" are the extension of a complex, developmental process that has its roots in systems ranging from cultures to social interactions.

Case Study: *Colin*

Colin is a seven-year-old boy who was referred to the psychology department of a major university medical center for evaluation. According to his mother, Colin presents numerous discipline problems at home and school, including fighting, disobedience, and defiance. He does not respond to his mother's harsh attempts to discipline him. Colin's mother self-referred to the county intensive home-based treatment program but does not comply with program requirements.

Two weeks after school started, Colin is suspended from elementary school for fighting. Colin is evaluated as somewhat small for his age, with little emotional expression or energy. The evaluator sees him as somewhat depressed. Six months earlier Colin moved to his mother's house from Oregon, where he was living with his father. His mother reports he had great difficulty adjusting to her care.

Colin's mother had become pregnant with Colin when she was 18 years old. She reports that she may have smoked marijuana during pregnancy and probably used amphetamines as well. Despite constant instability and moves during the pregnancy, Colin's mother describes her pregnancy as uneventful. Delivery was uncomplicated, but at the time Colin's mother and father were homeless and spent the early months of Colin's life living in a tent. At 2–3 months Colin contracted pneumonia, lost 11 pounds and coughed up blood. He was hospitalized in the intensive care unit for several weeks. Colin's mother reported he had always been a good eater, although food was sometimes scarce. He has had many ear infections. At seven Colin smokes cigarettes regularly. According to his mother, Colin reached most developmental milestones at the late end of the normal range. He spoke his first words at 18 months, ate by himself at two, and was toilet trained at two-and-a-half.

Colin's social history is marked by recurrent separations and questionable caregiving. He lived with his parents in a tent until he was 11 months old. At one year the family moved to California, and Colin's mother became pregnant with her second child, Ray. When she was eight months pregnant, mother and father separated. Two weeks after the birth of Ray, when Colin was approximately 20 months, mother, Colin, and Ray went to live with a girlfriend. The mother and old father reunited, and the family lived in a motel. Mother and father separated again, and mother returned to live with the girlfriend, then took an apartment with a male friend while Colin and Ray remained with the mother's girlfriend.

Several more separations and reunions took place until the mother took Colin and Ray to live with a boyfriend when Colin was two-and-a-half. When Colin was three, he and Ray were sent to live with his father in a logging camp in Washington. Mother reports knowledge of father's drug abuse and physical abuse of Colin during this period. She chose to take Ray to live with her and left Colin with father. Little is known about the period of Colin's life between ages three and seven, except suspected physical and sexual abuse of Colin and his father's history of drug abuse and violence. Colin returns to live with his mother in late spring when he has just turned seven. His mother is living with her boyfriend, who abuses alcohol and Percodan, and is physically abusive to Colin, although mother describes him as also loving of Colin.

Colin's mother's family history is marked by a number of life hazards as well. She is the oldest of four children and was adopted. She was raised on a farm by Christian parents, who were reportedly very affectionate toward her and never argued. Colin's mother reportedly felt lonely and isolated as a teenager and moved out of the home at 16. She married Colin's father when she was 18 because she was pregnant with Colin. Colin's mother describes a pattern of excessive drug use until age 25 and a history of involvement with abusive men.

Colin's father has a history of drug and alcohol use coupled with violent behavior. He has abused Colin's mother and several other girlfriends. He was himself physically and sexually abused by his father, and his mother is reported as being "crazier than a loon"; she would seduce men in front of Colin's father when he was boy.

What are the chances that this child would *not* get in a fight during the first two weeks of school? Where is the "risk" for this child, and can any of it be located within him? School personnel want him out of the school and in a full-day program for children with behavior disorders. Based on this case, how could disorder be defined? What processes and systems would be involved in preventive intervention for Colin? What do you think his life-course will look like?

part three

Schooling

8

What Do High-Risk Children Come To?

Contemporary Schools

The United States has more than 15,000 public school districts with more than 83,000 schools (Mattson, 1993). The local school district remains a uniquely independent political institution. In some states, for example, Wisconsin, school districts cross county lines. Districts vary markedly in size. Illinois, for example, has 964 districts, whereas Virginia, only slightly smaller in area and population has but 136 (Mattson, 1993). Some rural school districts may have but a single building and no high school, whereas 21 districts in this country have more than 100,000 students, ranging from Orange County, Florida (103,000), to New York City (943,969) (Editors of *Education Week*, 1993). Some states have statewide text book-adoption policies, thus insuring some commonality across districts. In other states texts are chosen at the district, school, or even classroom level.

Whatever the homogenizing effects of textbooks, standardized tests, and increasing state control, one must be cautious in speaking of the American school as though it were a single entity. One of us (Walsh) lives in a "twin city." One steps off the curb to cross the street and moves from Champaign to Urbana. One can move back and forth between cities without leaving the University library, but most who have had experience with both school districts agree that they are very different.

We ask, then, the readers' indulgence in the descriptions that we make below. Of necessity we overgeneralize and ignore the variation that exists across classrooms and schools, but there are identifiable commonalities in contemporary American schools.

AMERICANS AND THEIR SCHOOLS

Generally Americans like their schools, despite the political and other rhetoric. When Americans do discuss the need for improving schools, they agree on improvements like higher standards, more emphasis on basics, and more competition. Some Americans are dissatisfied with their schools but this "dissatisfaction with the educational system essentially as it stands rests primarily with the powerless—the poor, minorities, the young" (Clark & Astuto, 1988, p. 20). Groups, for example, from the religious right, may voice loud opposition to specific policies, for example, "family life" curricula. Recently protests have been mounted against Outcome Based Education (OBE). But generally Americans are supportive of their schools (Clark & Astuto, 1988).

Americans do not appear to be unequivocal in their financial support of their schools. The rhetoric of support for education that marked the national administrations of the past decade was seldom matched by actual monetary support. In fact, federal financial support for schools declined precipitously during the Reagan-Bush years (Verstegen, 1990). At the local level the failure to pass bond issues and tax levies becomes commonplace.

Rhetoric without actual financial support has made schooling an even riskier enterprise for many children than it had been previously. The decline in federal aid for schools, camouflaged by the shift to "block grants" to states, had the most telling effect on poor and minority children, as it was programs for these children that were most affected. In recent years, the passage of Public Laws 94-142 and 94-457 requiring local school districts to provide services to special-needs children from birth on, but providing no fiscal support to provide those services, has further drawn local resources away from the children of the poor and minorities.

This society takes a curious attitude toward the efficacy of schooling. Schools have always been a favorite target for critics and politicians. When times are bad we blame the schools. In 1983 when we were told that the nation was at risk, the blame was placed on the schools. Writes Gerald Bracey:

> Schools stink. Says who? Virtually everyone. When George Bush announced *America 2000*, he said that we've "moved beyond the days of issuing report after report about the dismal state of our schools." The opening sentence of Edward Fiske's recent book

is succinct; "It's no secret that America's public schools are failing." Chester Finn, former assistant secretary for research and improvement in the U.S. Department of Education, is no kinder: "[These] examples [of educational shortcomings] are so familiar.... (1991, p. 105)

Bracey goes on to argue, quite convincingly, that the "evidence over-whelmingly shows that *American schools have never achieved more than they currently achieve*. And some indicators show them performing better than ever" (p. 106). Westbury's (1992) reanalysis of the Second International Math Study (SIMS) shows that American students do not compare as unfavorably to Japanese students in math as we had been led to believe. In fact, they perform very similarly.

Ironically, although schools are regularly blamed for the nation's economic and other problems, they never receive credit for its successes. As Larry Cuban pointed out:

For the last decade, U.S. presidents, corporate leaders, and critics blasted public schools for a globally less competitive economy, sinking productivity, and jobs lost to other nations. The United States...had educationally disarmed itself in a hostile economic war. "If only to keep and improve on the slim competitive edge we still retain in world markets," [*A Nation At-Risk*] said, we must dedicate ourselves to the reform of our educational system.... Why is that now with a bustling economy, rising productivity, and shrinking unemployment American public schools are not receiving credit for the turn around? (1994, p. 44)

Schools, however, most certainly operate under strains and stresses that they have not faced in the past. Bracey (1992) expressed his astonishment that

Bush and the Secretary of Education rail at relatively small differences between the U.S. and other countries and maintain a stony silence on the enormous gaps between rich and poor students, between black and white students, and between Hispanic and white students right in our own backyard (p. 113).... The true crisis of education in America is that it is trying to function not only in an era of disinformation but also in a time of social decline that sometimes looks like collapse. (p. 115)

Bracey's point is compelling. Schools do not operate in vacuums. They are systems embedded in and connected with other systems. If, indeed, the larger culture is in a period of social decline, then schools will be directly and immediately affected. The larger culture is a super-ordinate system and as such regulates subordinate systems like schools.

The end result is that those children whose risk for school failure is already high will be affected; their risk will very likely increase. It may well be that American schools are not failing, but they are failing those children at the bottom—children at high risk of academic failure.

THE PERENNIAL AMERICAN SCHOOL: THE INSIDE

Children come to schools that are set in their ways and that have changed little over the century. Today's children are entering schools quite similar to the ones their parents, grandparents, and even great grandparents entered. Either our grandparents' schools were remarkably advanced, or our children's are a bit behind. If schools have not changed, the world in which those schools are located certainly has. Based on data gathered from over 1,000 elementary and secondary classrooms, Sirotnik found little variety in teaching practices across schools: "The majority of class time is spent in teachers lecturing to the class or in students working on written assignments.... We have seen that schools have changed little since we and those before us were there. What have [sic] changed, and what continue [sic] to change, are the economic, social, and political realities of the society in which we live" (1983, pp. 16–29).

Goodlad (1983a) concluded his major study of American schooling by arguing that the work of children and teachers in schools has not changed since the turn of the century. The classroom he describes is immediately recognizable to anyone who has spent much time, as most of us have, in American classrooms. "Teachers are in charge; they set the dominant tone. Students are passive. They listen and watch; they do written assignments and they take quizzes—lots of quizzes. There is little praise, little correction with feedback, little laughter, little anger, little overt emotionality of any kind. The tone of most classrooms in our sample is best described as flat" (pp. 795–796).

An image of school is deeply embedded in the American consciousness. A theme that runs through the literature on teacher training is that preservice teachers are more affected by how they were taught than by how they are trained to teach. It is difficult to sit at school board meetings, at faculty meetings in schools of education, anywhere in this county, as both of us have on many occasions, and not come away convinced that Americans believe that they know what schools are, how they should look, and how they should feel, even when they do not agree on details. People who run schools respond to those images and struggle to maintain schools that are recognizable to their constituents. Walsh (1993) concluded in his study of school change that much opposition to changes in classroom practice had less to do with what was occurring in the classrooms than it did with the fact the classrooms looked different from the classrooms that oppositional adults remembered, or at least believe they remembered, from their youth.

Schools remain recognizable. They have principals and teachers, classrooms and gyms, or multipurpose rooms that double as lunchrooms and gyms. The front doors have signs welcoming visitors but reminding them to sign in at the office, which is usually located just inside the front door. Schools are not unfriendly, but they seldom feel truly welcoming to the visitor. Certainly many parents of high-risk children do not see schools as welcoming.

Inside there are hallways to walk down—walk, don't run, in line, close to the walls—lined with bulletin boards, usually colorful, at times cute, less often attractive or artistic. Off the hallways are classrooms, with numbers and teachers' names on the doors, and lavatories and janitor's closets. Schools look like schools.

To the extent that schools are changing, they appear to be advancing torward more rigid systems. Consider in recent years the increased emphasis in testing children and grouping them, even "preflunking" (Ellwein et al., 1991; Shepard & Smith, 1989; Walsh, Ellwein, Eads, & Miller, 1991) them even before they enter school. Were the screening being done for diagnostic purposes to help schools understand how best to respond to children, to facilitate their learning, one might defend this trend. But the evidence mounts (Durkin, 1987; Walsh, 1989) that for all the early testing that is being done in this country, little if any is being used for diagnostic purposes. Rather it is being done to sort and select.

Schools give more high-stakes tests, tests that must be passed in order to move to the next level of schooling or to graduate. An extreme version of this type of testing was a first-grade "entrance exam" implemented in one state. The positive effects of high-stakes tests have been forcefully debunked (e.g., Ellwein & Glass, 1989).

In early schooling the most notable change has been the rapid and large rise in retention rates in kindergarten and first grade (Shepard & Smith, 1989; Walsh, 1989; Walsh et al., 1992), a practice that appeals to the "get tough" mentality that seems always to lurk on the edges of discussions of what needs to be done with schools. Retention, nevertheless, has been unequivocally shown to have few positive effects and many negative ones (Holmes, 1989; Holmes & Matthews, 1984; Jackson, 1975).

Children are coming to schools that resemble the ones their parents went to, except they are more rigid. If they are not more test driven, one may conclude that the testing is occurring earlier and earlier. Resnick and Resnick observed: "American school children are the most tested in the world and the least examined. We distinguish here between examinations as formal inquires into the extent to which students have mastered a particular curriculum and tests as assessments only loosely linked to what is taught in any particular school" (1985, p. 17).

Teachers

When children enter the classroom, they encounter a teacher who, like them, is encountering an increasing number of hazards in her (inevitably the teacher is female) personal and professional life. She is white, a woman, and has been teaching for 10–20 years. In 1990 she was one of 2,401,000 public school elementary and secondary teachers. She made $33,015 in 1989–1990. Although 86% of teachers expressed a "degree of satisfaction with their jobs…only 20 to 30% say they would become teachers if they had to start over again" (Mattson, 1993, pp. 6.2–6.3).

Goodlad (1983b) argued that "teaching is still a highly individualistic, isolated endeavor. The teacher closes the door and does what he or she pleases" (p. 56). Nevertheless, the evidence mounts that the teacher has little control of her classroom curriculum, and what control she has is waning. Instead texts (Apple, 1986), state mandates, micromanaging school boards (Cuban, 1976), regulations, parental demands, and principals still flexing their muscles from the afterglow of the effective-schools movement direct them and constrain them.

The teacher struggles with a history, personally and professionally, of being undervalued and overdirected. "Throughout most of American History, however, teachers have constituted more of a procession than a profession…. Much of the nostalgia for the good old days of teaching is, in my view, misplaced, if not plain wrong" (Tyack, 1987, p. 171).

Other historians, notably Herbst in his book *And Sadly Teach* (1989), concur. Herbst described the historical realities of teaching by comparing teachers to their students: "[l]ike their students, teachers are to be seen in school, but…not to raise their voices" (p. 3).

Many teachers are dedicated to their work. They struggle with their attitudes and care for the children they teach. One of us (Walsh) has worked closely with teachers in his research over the past 7 years and has witnessed remarkable individuals and groups of individuals in their work, teachers who have, for example, built up personal libraries of 3,000 trade books in their classrooms, who create classrooms "notable for an atmosphere...that is sensitive to children, to individual needs, to individual decision-making, and to choice in learning" (Harp, 1993, p.1). [For a wonderful description of such a classroom see Shelor, (1993).]

Still teachers have had to struggle with being typified as weak intellectually and otherwise. They are told that they are, for example, conceptually simplistic (Jackson, 1968), oriented to the concrete and the practical (Doyle & Ponder, 1977–1978). Increasingly researchers have begun to look more carefully and have found capable and honest human beings. To give just a few examples of researchers looking very closely at teachers of young children, Walsh, Baturka, Smith, and Colter (1991) showed a teacher negotiating curricular and personal change with remarkable sophistication and honesty. Ayers (1989) constructed compelling portraits of six preschool teachers, bringing the reader into their lives as teachers. Vasconcelos (1995) brought to life a preschool teacher whose teaching continues the development of democracy in Portugal. Wolf (1995) showed how teacher-caregivers in a small town day-care center struggled for some control in a context in which they had very little. Ceglowski (1995) described the efforts of Head Start teachers to enact policies at the local level made by bureaucrats far removed from the classroom and the poor rural children found there. Lee (1995) detailed the efforts of university laboratory preschool teachers to straddle the very different worlds of the university and the preschool.

Haller (1985) showed that the naive charges of bigotry that have plagued teachers are inaccurate. Natriello and Dornbusch (1983) concluded their study by arguing: "In contrast with studies which portray teachers as indulging their prejudices, our studies indicate that teachers behave rationally in their interactions with students with different characteristics as they use available information to formulate appropriate responses to students in classrooms" (p. 29).

Over the years the teacher has seen many changes in the school population. More children are coming from families in which both parents are working; more children come from single-parent families. The teacher may have seen the urban neighborhood change from white-middle class affluence to minority poverty or something in-between. She may have seen her small rural town slowly begin to disappear or mutate into a suburb or a bedroom community. And during the 15 or so years she has been a teacher, she has seen countless educational fads come and go. She can remember the confusion of the new math, which disappeared as quickly as it came. She has been through a number of principals, more superintendents, each with a different agenda. Through it all she has maintained an enduring vision of school, learning, in the words of one teacher, "This, too, shall pass" (Walsh et al., 1991).

She has become accustomed to many people telling her what to do, successions of many people telling her what to do, each year a new supervisor working her or his way up the bureaucracy. Consider the words of one experienced teacher. "So much of my career was having somebody tell me what to say, how to behave, where to go, what to do. That's the book on being a teacher. Having to be in a constant position of groveling" (Walsh, 1995).

No one who has spent any time in schools would deny that there are mean-spirited, lazy, and poorly prepared teachers who should be counseled rapidly into other professions, if not other solar systems. If such people exist, and certainly they do, they will be represented in schools. Rather our point is that there are many who are hardworking, caring, and knowledgeable, and more importantly, that teaching is a very human profession and that the teacher's role in schooling must be understood as a very complex, difficult, and multifaceted one. Schools remain challenging places for well-intentioned, knowledgeable, and talented people to do good things.

The teachers in this county are aging. As noted earlier, the teacher has been working from 10 to 20 years. Many graduated from college in the heyday of behaviorism's influence in schools of education. The teacher was inducted into the language of behavioral objectives and reinforcement, as, quite likely was her principal and many of the aging central office staff who should support her but more likely supervise her. She was taught to teach by direct instruction and to group children by ability. She may have had an introduction to Piagetian constructivism, which was probably vulgar-Piaget with an emphasis on stages, but it is unlikely that she was exposed to developmental perspectives during her training. She may have a masters degree—40% do (Mattson, 1993), but how much she has continued her education probably depends on state and local requirements for maintaining certification and on her own personal desire to continue her education.

Her training, like that of her younger colleagues, was disproportionately pedagogical, with relatively little attention paid to theories of development. Theories of learning were presented separately from theories of development, or if the behaviorist influence was strong enough, as one and the same thing.

Early-childhood teachers who see themselves as "developmental" might object to this portrayal, but the dominant developmentalism of the early-childhood world has as much in common with the maturationist theories of the early 20th century as with the Piagetian theory with which it claims affiliation. It has little at all to do with the systems approach presented in this volume.

Consequently today's practitioner is more likely to operate within a management-oriented framework than a developmental one. Her attention has been focused by her training and by those who supervise her on increasing student performance, managing behavior, and using techniques that stimulate or diminish certain student outputs or behaviors. This orientation does not attend to the underlying meaning of behaviors, the developmental antecedents of behaviors, the ecological contexts in which these behaviors are developed and maintained. Neither she, her supervisors, nor most of her professors are familiar with the recent literature on development, for example, developmental psychopathology or post-Piagetian developmental theory, which has enormous implications for the kinds of environments and experiences afforded children through the public schools (Pianta & Nimitz, 1989).

THE OUTSIDE: LOCAL POLITICS

The child also enters a school that is deeply embedded, even embroiled, in politics. At the local level, it is run by what Cuban called "archaic forms of governance layers designed for village schools" (1976, p. 112). It would not be an exaggeration to look at the history of American schools as a history of struggle between school boards and administrators. In the process teachers have found themselves in the middle of endless, and seemingly pointless, tugs of war, being pulled first this way and then that.

School boards, since their inception, have been involved in what critics call "micromanagement," that is, becoming engaged in the day-to-day administration of the schools, something they are not now nor have they ever been empowered to do. Cuban (1976) describes reformers in 1880 attacking boards for interfering in superintendents' business, haggling over which grammar book or method of penmanship to use, whether new desks should be of maple or oak (1976, p. 113). This criticism continues today. In the 1930s Charles Judd argued for the abolition of school boards in order to bypass the vagaries of local politics (Tyack & Hansot, 1982, p. 132). During the years after World War II, the Japanese accepted all manner of American-imposed institutions, except for one, the school board, which they felt would create inequities.

Some critics are kinder. One community leader was quoted as saying, "The board is made up of basically good intentioned people, but they don't have the experience or backgrounds to deal with complex issues" (The Institute for Educational Leadership, 1986).

The picture that critics, kind and otherwise, draw of school boards is of groups of people caught in the vagaries of local politics, dependent on powerful patrons (in many areas, becoming a board member is seen as entry into a career in politics), lacking the experience to do the complex job they have to do, and becoming obsessed with running the schools on a day-to-day details basis.

Our point is that school boards are often an immediate source of stress for those attempting to run schools. Callahan's (1962) well-regarded historical tale tells of superintendents' caving into the pressures for social efficiency and scientific management in attempts to keep their jobs in a business-dominated, efficiency-conscious society, but nevertheless still losing those jobs with remarkable regularity. Gross (1958) described the pressures that superintendents are under daily in great detail. At times one is left wondering why anyone would desire such a position. As we wrote the first draft of this chapter, the superintendency of the Los Angeles public schools was open. Would anyone, we wondered, actually take it? In fact, in 1990, 20 of the 25 superintendencies in the largest urban school districts were vacant (Olson & Bradley, 1992)

Tyack and Hansot relate an account of a superintendent's efforts to deal with his school board's desire to maintain complete control of the schools. Frank Cody was appointed superintendent of the Detroit schools in 1919 and held the job for many years. The day he was appointed a male board member visited him and said, "Frank, each morning I want you to come over to my office and tell me of your plans for the day before you take any action." "I'll do better than that," said Cody, "I'll come over and kiss you good morning" (1982, p. 144).

Superintendents, like everyone who works in the schools, are under pressures. The pressures they feel make their way into the classroom. These pressures constrain superintendents, principals, teachers, and eventually children.

Patterns of interactions are the fabric of the school culture. One clear pattern of interaction in schools, which are very hierarchical systems, is that everyone has someone telling him or her what to do—school boards direct superintendents, who direct assistants and principals, who direct teachers, who direct children. The relationships are extremely asymmetrical and highly regulated. They become more asymmetrical and more regulated the further down the system one goes. Missing are mechanisms for feedback and necessary levels of mutuality.

Pressures that enter the system at the top are unlikely to be diffused but instead will make their way rapidly down to the bottom. At the very bottom of this asymmetric, highly regulated system are high-risk children.

9

Conversations Between Children and Schools

From the ground up makes good sense for building. Beware of from the top down.

—Frank Lloyd Wright

This past May I (DJW) waited in my car to pick up my daughter on her last day of second grade. Her teacher walked her slowly across the playground, and at first I wondered why. Not until they came close could I see that my daughter was crying uncontrollably. She was distraught that she would be leaving her teacher of two years. "All the girls," she later told me, "were crying. And the boys were all fighting hard to hold back their tears."

If schools were to become places to which children were happy to go in the morning and which they were sad to leave at the end of the year, we would have made great progress in addressing the problem of unacceptably high risk. Schools do very well by the top third of students, and even the middle third are served. But we fail with the remaining students, the bottom third. Ultimately, some form of intentional, directed change is necessary to improve the conversation between child/family and schooling for the bottom third (Comer, 1988).

CHANGE AND SCHOOLING

Schools cannot change society. They are but part of the larger system and have limited resources to direct toward changing dysfunctional relationships within or between family, community, or culture. But schools play an important role in maintaining health in a cultural system. Furthermore, changes can be made in schools that will positively affect the lives of children who attend them. For example, small improvements in communication between teacher and parent can benefit the child immensely. In the Contextual Systems Model, the starting point for change of this sort is how schools see the children who come to them. Catherine Taylor stated our position most eloquently.

> Ultimately, if real change is to take place in the quality of students as they leave our schools, we have to make real changes in our beliefs about learners. We must begin to believe that *most* students are quite capable of learning and achieving; that the dramatic differences we see in student performance are the result of conditions unrelated to students' capacity to learn.… [But] we cannot ignore the dramatic differences between children as they enter school. We will have to face the fact that not all students are equally open to learning. We will have to accept that not all students are equally prepared to learn; that some are learning despite dramatic obstacles while others are nurtured by supportive environments. (1994, p. 255)

But the task of change is made more difficult by chronic skepticism regarding schools' ability to change to meet the shifting needs of society. Consider one review of the efforts at school reform.

> John Goodlad, in reviewing major educational reform efforts, maintains that the work of teachers and students has hardly changed since the turn of the century. Arno Bellack argues convincingly that the most interesting phenomenon of reform is the schools' remarkable resistance to change. Stability, not change, seems to be the dominant characteristic. Thomas Romberg, from an analysis of one reform effort, states that most change, however well intended, ends up being nominal (with changes in labels, but not practice). From a case study, Neal Gross demonstrated how enthusiasms and dedication erode over a very short time when practitioners revert to old habits. (Romberg & Price, 1983, p. 160)

These results are as much a function of the kinds of reforms implemented and the way they were carried out as of resistance to change peculiar to schools or educators. It seems unlikely that educators are more reluctant to change than are other groups in society. As Walsh, Baturka, et al., (1991) wrote:

> We strongly question this whole attitude [that teachers are resistant to change]. We do not believe researchers looked carefully enough, or with enough respect. Change is a very complex slow process that any reasonable person negotiates with care. People have strongly felt convictions. One does not spend years defining oneself

and making sense out of one's world only to abandon one's identity because a bureaucrat has decided that it is time to do something else. (p. 85)

Educators, like anyone else, will change when it makes sense for them to change, when the proposed change can be incorporated into their personal and professional identities, and when the support necessary to make the changes is provided. Profound and successful efforts at school reform have been documented (e.g., Brown, 1991; Comer, 1980, 1985, 1988; Tharp & Gallimore, 1988; Walsh, 1993).

Contrary to skeptics who argue that little has changed, or can change, in education, the Contextual Systems Model suggests that change is actually occuring all the time, in the co-action between and among interacting systems. In fact, schooling has changed dramatically in the last century and in the last 20 years. The problem is that the output of these changed schools (student achievement) has not matched social expectations. Change is an inevitable consequence of development. From the perspective of the Contextual Systems Model, reform is an attempt to strategically direct development. Attempts to change schools must come to grips with the principles of change in developmental systems, and "see" these principles at work in reform efforts. Fundamental to this discussion is an appreciation of social processes in schools. Social processes and interactions between and among systems create the "structures" that change efforts either harness intentionally or butt up against. These processes function with respect to rules: self-stabilization, self-reorganization, and homeostasis all refer to how codes that regulate system interactions change as a function of exposure to new elements.

Systems theory suggests the process of change is going to be slow and iterative—with lots of circling back. Systems do not reorganize (e.g., become noticeably different) quickly. Instead, systems change as a function of continual microchanges that reflect small, ongoing adaptations. Over time, these small adaptations produce reorganization—this occurs with respect to the development of any system—children, classrooms, teaching, schools. But the quick-fix approach has long plagued American schooling.

SCHOOLS AS SOCIAL SYSTEMS

We started this book with the goal of advancing discourse on children who are highly likely to fail at the demands of public education. In particular, we took as our focus the relationship between two systems: one encompassing the child and home/family, and the other encompassing the school as a setting and as a process. Risk is not located in any single corner of these systems—not in the child, the family, or the school, and the solutions for risk are not to be found in any single location—child, teacher, classroom, family. Risk is distributed across all aspects of these systems, and the larger systems of community and society.

Social Process vs. Social Structure

Schools are social places, and schooling is a social process. Social processes regulate how risk develops and ultimately becomes manifest in a child's adaptation to school. The child comes to school from a web of relationships with parents, peers, and neighborhood, which yields patterns of interactions that will be brought into play in the classroom. Classroom experiences and expectations will activate these patterns of interaction, directly and indirectly. The child's actions, which are based on these patterns of interactions, will elicit various reactions from adults and children, again very much based on their own patterns of interactions.

How individuals in the school respond to the child has a major effect on how the child fits in the school and classroom, the degree to which she or he belongs. We know, for example, that the variation in children's actual classroom behavior is different and not as broad as the variation in teacher-child relationships (Pianta, 1994). However else one defines schooling, especially in the very early years, it is mostly about face-to-face interaction between children and adults, and these interactions, these *conversations*, are the process of adjustment, or adaptation. Test scores and other common assessment measures are but blurry snapshots of this process.

Many explanations of risk and school adaptation adopt a non-process-oriented view, however. Adjustment and adaptation are defined by test scores and demographic marker variables (socioeconomic status, gender). To the extent that these definitions of adjustment drive policy, research, and educational programs that address risk, the actual experiences of children in school will change very little as a function of these policies, practices, and research. We no longer really believe that we can teach the children of the poor, or worse, that the children of the poor can learn.

As our society grows increasingly complex, the social structure explanations that have dominated the discourse on schooling for decades are less useful (see chapter 2). Children in this society grow up in a diversity of contexts. Grand markers like socioeconomic status are less useful as society diversifies. A focus on social processes within broad marker variables unveils the risk and protective mechanisms that can then inform the next generation of process-oriented reform (Reid, 1994). For example, most developed nations have been able to unlink the relation between low socioeconomic status and low achievement. American society has not.

In fact, one reason that socioeconomic status is so strongly linked to low achievement is that social processes in schools are not highly diverse. As was noted in chapter 8, schools are highly regimented settings—curriculum varies little across and within classrooms, and practice is dominated by codes for regulating behavior and interactions among children, teachers, and staff. Yet children enter schools from contextual systems in which the nature of interaction among children, adults, and social systems has a staggering range. There are many kinds of children, or better, all children can be many kinds of children over the course of their lives, but there is one kind of school, in which far too few children do well over the entire course of their education.

That poverty, or any other structural variable, predicts with some degree of efficiency an outcome in schools as they now exist does not guarantee that it will predict as well in other versions of school. In fact it does not (e.g., Comer, 1985; 1988; Holtzmann, 1992). Further, poverty could continue to be a strong predictor in that children would still line up the same way, with poorer children still not doing as well as their more affluent peers, but variation in social processes in the classroom could shift and compress the range of achievement such that the average would be higher. The problem is not so much who is at the bottom, but where the bottom is located. Right now the bottom is at the rock-bottom level.

Schools As Systems

If nothing else, the Contextual Systems Model embraces the fact that multiple agents, or systems, constrain the development of the child—either in or out of school. A lens that focuses on single factors has little or no contribution to make to understanding or improving schooling. The principle of holism calls attention to the fact that the activity of any agent or system within a matrix of interacting systems has meaning only with respect to its relation to the whole. Efforts at changing schools, classrooms, or achievement are subject to this principle. Yet the principle is consistently violated or ignored in educational reform. It has been suggested, for example, that children go to school more hours per day and more days per year, without considering the contemporary realities of children who already are institutionalized in before-school programs, after-school programs, and daycare, more hours per day and more days per year than previous generations (National Research Council, 1990). Thus interventions are suggested without considering the whole.

The search for "best practices" or "alternative practices" that can be the basis of reform and intervention also falls prey to a focus on single factors. When appeals are made, for example, for U. S. schools to emulate Japanese schools (because longer days and school years are correlated with higher achievement), ignored is any sense of the larger cultural whole or other aspects of schooling there. Ignored is the Japanese emphasis on the group and the lack of emphasis on individual ability, the fact that schools are organized to maximize high-quality instruction—teachers do not spend time collecting lunch money; they are given time to prepare, to observe master teachers, and new teachers serve an extended apprenticeship period. Ignored also are little details like the generous amount of recess that Japanese students have and the amount of time spent on nonacademic activities (Lewis, 1995). Nor is mention made of the more problematic aspects of Japanese education—once in college students seldom study, or even go to class. Instead, it is all very simple—the Japanese do better because they go to school more.

Schools are social systems. They deal in the currency of interactions among individuals, groups, and institutions. And school behavior cannot be explained by single variables. From these basic facts a number of implications for policy, practice, and research emerged, these are contained within the Contextual Systems Model.

APPLICATIONS OF THE CONTEXTUAL SYSTEMS MODEL TO SCHOOLING

A focus on protective and vulnerability mechanisms yields a rich description of the processes involved in the manufacturing of risk (Rutter, 1987). As described by Rutter, protective and vulnerability mechanisms reflect a response to a risk situation or risk exposure, "a modification of a person's response to risk" (p. 317). Protective mechanisms operate to ameliorate or reduce the reaction to risk factors that in ordinary circumstances lead to negative outcomes (for the child). Vulnerability mechanisms intensify the reaction to risk, leaving risk unchallenged and unchecked, with the probability of negative outcomes becoming increasingly high.

The specification of protection and vulnerability processes is important for describing the various roles that schools or classrooms may play in interaction with family and community, to increase or decrease the relative risk of a given student. Schools can be places in which protective mechanisms operate. For example, several studies demonstrate the positive effects of structured, supported interactions with peers (and teachers) on the social behavior of children at high risk for learning and behavior problems (Conduct Problems Prevention Research Group, 1992; Pianta, Steinberg, & Rollins, 1995) and the negative effects of certain retention practices (Shepard & Smith, 1989; Walsh et al., 1992).

A striking example of long-term protective process is provided by the studies showing positive long-term effects of high-quality preschool intervention (Lazar, Darlington, Murray, Royce, & Snipper, 1982; Schweinhart, Barnes, & Weikart, 1993). Children who had been in these programs did not show large intelligence quotient (IQ) or academic gains but rather the ability to function successfully in school (they were retained and placed in special education less frequently than controls) and later in society (they were less often arrested and on welfare). Preschool experience clearly has a protective effect on the process of development in high-risk students (Ramey & Campbell, 1991).

Ramey and Campbell (1991) and Garmezy (1984) call attention to protective mechanisms at work in school programs. Several factors repeatedly are associated with positive outcomes in high-risk children: (a) positive personal characteristics of the child (sociable, even-tempered, intelligent); (b) a supportive relationship with an adult or older peer (e.g., teacher, parent, sibling); and (c) an extended social network that supports the child's efforts to cope with stress (e.g., involvement between school and home, participation in community groups, church). These protective factors moderate the effects of stress exposure by interrupting the link between initial exposure to stress or risk conditions and subsequent exposures to additional stressors. By interrupting this link and introducing new links to supportive elements, these factors divert developmental trajectories that otherwise would be directed toward negative outcomes.

The Contextual Systems Model advances the goal of schools' attaining the status of protective mechanisms—places and systems through which risk is reduced. The emphasis on process and linkages in schooling and the school as a context for learning and development create a conceptual framework that moves toward prevention and away from intervention (Pianta, 1990). Thus the applications of the Contextual

Systems Model are largely focused on processes that occur in developmental systems, drawn from the discussions of Systems Theory and development in chapters 4, 5, and 6.

Asymmetric Relationships and Development

One unifying theme from the Contextual Systems Perspective is that in *developmental* systems, immature organisms are placed in contact with mature organisms in asymmetric relationships. The asymmetry of these relationships places responsibility for regulation of development on the superordinate, or more mature system. In this discussion responsibility refers to the fact that the outcomes associated with this system are in large part a function of the behavior of the more mature organism (Ford & Lerner, 1992; Sroufe, 1989). Prominent among these are relationships children have with parents. Schools are involved in many asymmetric relationships with children: teacher-child, school-teacher, superintendent-principal, school-child, classroom-child. In each of these, the "responsible" system is listed first.

These asymmetric relationships advance development in many ways through countless interactions, structuring of activity, and introduction of new information and challenges to the immature, developing system. As noted above, because the relationship is asymmetric, greater responsibility resides with the more mature or superordinate partner for regulation of developmental activity within the relationship. In dyadic systems such as parent-child, the less mature organism will become only as organized as the superordinate system (Greenspan, 1989).

Many developmental theorists argue (Sander, 1975; Sroufe, 1989) that the organization of the child mirrors the organization found in the relationship between the child and caregiver. It is for this reason that the superordinate system (parent, teacher, school) has a disproportionate responsibility for development. Thus if children are to solve problems flexibly and self-reliantly, or cope with stresses and strains with self-control and the use of representational symbols (see chapter 6), then schools must operate at the same level of organization present in these processes (Greenspan, 1989). If schooling processes are reflexive, reactive, overly rigid or nonsymbolic, then the developing systems within them (e.g., children) will operate at the same level of organization.

Relationships with Teachers

One asymmetric relationship within the school that can promote development is a relationship with a teacher (Sroufe, 1983). As many practitioners know, the social and affective interaction taking place in classrooms is of primary importance in determining who succeeds and who fails, especially for students whose background characteristics are indicative of a lack of social and affective resources. As empahsized earlier, these processes, not socioeconomic status, may be fundamental to understanding the school as a context for development.

Werner and Smith (1982) studied a sample of poor children and determined that one of the factors accounting for positive outcomes among these high-risk children was a supportive relationship with a teacher. These relationships prevented many of the outcomes (e.g., dropping out, behavior problems and psychopathology, academic failure) that plague American schools today. Pianta and colleagues (1995) have shown that patterns of teacher-child relationships in kindergarten (e.g., conflicted, open/close, and dependent) are predictive of subsequent school adjustment and, for high-risk children, related to positive and negative outcomes.

Teachers' responses to child-initiated relationship behaviors appear influential in determining classroom adjustment. Pederson, Faucher, and Eaton (1978), in a case study of a first-grade teacher, show the impact of a teacher who formed relationships with students that made them feel worthwhile, supported their independence, motivated them to achieve, and provided them with support to interpret and cope with environmental demands. The combination of felt security in a relationship with an adult and freedom to explore the world in a competent manner is a hallmark of the parent-child attachment; it appears to also operate within the teacher-child relationship. This teachers' students differed from their same-age peers on dropout rates, academic achievement, behavioral competence, and adjustment in the adult world.

Boyer (1983) notes that a relationship with a supportive teacher is a major factor associated with prevention of dropouts. The social and relational nature of risk is underscored by the backgrounds of students who fail in school. These students often have experienced considerable relationship stress: for example, divorce, child maltreatment, or parental depression. Healthy teacher-child relationships appear to help ameliorate the negative consequences of these experiences.

But teacher-child relationships act as protective mechanisms for high-risk children only when they mirror the kind of sensitive, mutual interactions that regulate development in positive parent-child relationships. This is not to say that teachers become like parents, instead, that teacher-child interactions possess the qualities of good parent-child interactions, including sensitive responsiveness by the adult and clear, contingent feedback.

One lesson derived from research on teacher-child relationships is the need to make schools less formal in their management of social interactions between teachers and children. Supportive asymmetric relationships fuel developmental change. Yet, much of what passes for structure in today's schools are attempts to formalize social exchanges into more rigid, tightly constrained formats. Consequently, social interactions cannot aide development. One distinct advantage of Developmentally Appropriate Practice is to call attention to the lifting of these constraints.

Again, process is more important than structure. Although teacher/student ratios are important, Tobin (1992) argues the present discussion of ratios insists on static, the-lower-the-better ratios. Thus, we want ratios of 1 to 6 or 1 to 10 depending on children's age, and this ratio remains stable across the school day, always one teacher with x number of children. In fact, it may well be that there are situations in which a ratio of 1 to 30 or more is not only more than adequate but also beneficial to the child, and other situations in which ratios of 1 to 2 or 3 are needed.

As teachers interact with children, so do teachers interact with principals, principals with superintendents, and superintendents with school boards. As pointed out in chapter 8, these interactions take place in asymmetric relationships, and nearly mirror one another. The codes that regulate behavior of superintendents when interacting with a school board are fairly similar to those that regulate teachers' behavior with principals. Interaction frequently consists of rigid regulatory behaviors on the part of the superordinate system that are aimed at constraining the behavior of the subordinate member of the relationship. In this way, creativity is stifled, solutions to problems are very limited, and roles are fairly fixed. This is why schools look similar and appear not to change. Lifting these kinds of constraints creates a more open relationship, or open system for regulating activity. Reorganization, change, and development are more likely in an open system. Successful reform efforts all find ways to lift constraints on "subordinate" systems and create more flexible, open systems for activity (e.g., Comer, 1988; Holtzmann, 1992; Schorr et al., 1991).

Integration and Differentiation

Another overarching theme derived from a Contextual Systems Model analysis of schooling is that schools (and homes and other systems) are overdifferentiated. There are too many people, too many contexts, too many differing demands, at too many times in children's lives for children to make any sense of what they are to do when they are in school. The systems responsible for regulating their activity are fragmented, unintegrated, chaotic, and disorganized. Overdifferentiation is present in several areas: (a) between child/family and school/schooling, (b) between school/schooling and other resources that can be used to support development of children, (c) within the classroom, and (d) with respect to time. In these overdifferentiated systems, boundaries are too many and often are rigidly maintained. Conversations, as implied by the Contextual Systems Model, are the integrative processes that cross boundaries to create shared meaning and goals. Overdifferentiated systems make conversations extremely difficult.

A Belonging Relationship with the School

An important conversation needs to take place between high-risk children and the school. Because of the subordinate nature of the child within the school, the responsibility for this conversation rests with the school and its personnel.

One hears often that schools need to be welcoming environments in which children feel safe, comfortable, and cared for. These notions are often applied to the youngest children, or to programs that enhance self-esteem. But all children deserve to "belong" in school; they deserve "membership" (Whelage et al., 1988). They have the right to an education, to be accepted in school, not to be shuttled off to the side and be complained about. The notion of belonging is an extension of the emphasis on "fit" that calls attention to the degree to which integrative links across systems make it possible for children to adapt in the school context. Belonging characterizes the quality of this relationship both from the perspective of the child and family, and from the perspective of the school. Belonging takes place as a function of conversations that cross system boundaries to result in shared meaning and goals.

In the Contextual Systems Model, child/family and school/schooling are complex systems composed of many subordinate systems and units, all of which are placed in dynamic interaction with one another. Boundaries between units and systems control the exchange of information, currency, energy, and resources across systems (Ford & Ford, 1987). When boundaries constrict connections across a large number of units, the organization of these units becomes highly differentiated and lacks the integrating links that allow resources to flow easily. Lacking integration, such systems become inflexible and maladaptive.

We have argued that "risk" exists in systems in which this type of overdifferentiation exists, in which the child is the *only* unit that flows across the boundaries of classrooms, or of home-school, and neighborhood-school. Schools in which the child is the only connection to systems outside of school are schools in which the child does not *belong*. Such schools are unmanageable systems, easily overwhelming the child's capacity to adapt. One conclusion to be drawn from this perspective is that schools (at *all* levels) need to create mini-systems that are more accessible and manageable. This is *critical* for the child for whom few links exist between home and school, or where home entails considerable hazards. As a child's risk coefficient rises, the school has to become proportionately more manageable for the child.

Schools in which children experience a sense of belonging are those that are integrated with community, home, and neighborhood; here the codes that regulate behavior are transferable across system boundaries, and responsibility for maintaining the relationship across these systems is *not* the child's but resides within the adults and institutions responsible for the child's welfare.

A group of reformers in San Antonio (Lein, Radle, & Radle, 1992) interviewed parents of elementary-school children in a poor housing-project school. Parents identified the following as priorities for improving schooling for their children: more information on what children are actually learning, more parent-teacher conferences, more intensive and inclusive Parent-Teacher Association (PTA) activities, improvements to the schools' physical environment, assistance in dealing with discipline problems, assistance in dealing with gang influence, graduate-equivalency degree (GED) classes, help on issues of housing, and avoidance of violence in the home.

Overall, parents wanted teachers to challenge their children in the classroom and they themselves wanted to be more involved in their child's education. The parents expected teachers, and the school as an institution, to develop higher expectations for their children. These eight priorities have to do with issues between home and school; home-school conversations.

These parent-stated needs are about creating a matrix of links between school and home—expectations, communication, interactions—that make school a knowable and understandable environment for children. Furthermore, the onus of responsibility for these conversations does not rest with the child. As discussed before, in many high-risk situations the child is the only contact between home and school and often has responsibility for that contact. Such an arrangement is counter-developmental.

Examples of systems in which conversations result in belonging are not infrequent, but are often not very visible. Comer's model of school change exemplifies the concept of belonging (Comer 1985, 1988), in which the school system actively opens itself to links with the family system of the children it educates. Schorr et al. (1991) document a number of representative programs that actively build links across school/home contexts; successful developmental outcomes can be attributed to these links.

Conversations provide the social process by which school is an understandable and accessible context for the child. Absent conversation, the child wanders aimlessly into a context that has little or no affordance value, no matter how stimulating, exciting, or self-esteem promoting it might see itself as being. The nature of belonging derives from the child's experience of familiarity and fit—codes for behavior and expectations are communicated and understandable, they recognize prior history and experience, they are consistent with the skills the child brings to school, and they offer comfort to the uncertainty of crossing the boundary into school. In very practical terms, a child who belongs knows what her or his relationship is with everyone in the school, janitor to principal, and this child knows that all those relationships are supportive of her or him.

Finally, conversations start with listening. The asymmetry of the child-school relationship requires that the school listen first, and listen attentively—not with filters that select only the information that is consistent with the present structure of the school, but with openness that allows information about the child to flow and be understood. Much of what passes for listening by schools are processes that reify the perception that risk resides somewhere in one of the corners of the invidious triangle: in the child's head, in the family, or in the school.

One way that schooling fails to listen to the child is by high-stakes testing of children (Meisels, 1987). High-stakes testing fails to promote listening in two ways (1) it focuses on discrete behaviors, carving up the child's capacities into discrete products, and (2) it fails to recognize the role of context in judgments about child competence.

As has been argued before, the developmental level of a child cannot be viewed solely in terms of discrete behaviors within one or another domain of development (Greenspan & Greenspan, 1991). Instead, developmental level is indexed by how capacities are organized to produce patterns of adaptive responses to salient developmental challenges. A child cannot be judged competent or not on the basis of behavior on any test. Instead, development must be examined in terms of how the resources of the child and context are organized to respond to problems (Resnick, 1994; Rogoff, 1990). This perspective has serious implications for the kinds of procedures most commonly used to make judgments about children's performance in school, almost all of which are based primarily on the child's performance in isolated domains and without regard for context.

The vast majority of assessment, evaluation, and testing procedures rely nearly entirely on descriptions of the child and his or her abilities independent from context, not as distributed within and across contexts (e.g., Martin, 1988). Children perform items either correctly or incorrectly. Children are rated or described in terms of abilities and disabilities, strengths and weaknesses, all of which are seen as located somewhere within them. These behaviors, abilities, and weaknesses typically are not located somewhere in the interaction of that child with a teacher, a school day, a family, a curriculum, or a peer group. Yet those interactions sustain performance, even on a single item on a single test. Then the results of testing are communicated in terms that reify the notion that skill is located within a child and not in an interaction, that learning processes are located in a child's head, and that the reason children do not perform well in a classroom has nothing to do with interactions but with how some section of their brain works (Riccio et al., 1993). Hogwash! (we use the term in its technical, scientific sense), brain activity is correlated with performance, and correlations are not causal (Greenough & Black, 1991).

The reliance on tests to ascertain individual abilities and disabilities and the use of these tests to link children to services seriously undermines the capacity of the school to listen, and then respond, to the child as an integrated whole. In this context, conversations will be constricted, distorted, and unidirectional (from school to child). In systems terms, feed-back and feed-forward functions will cease to function in a way that maintains balanced interactions and free information flow. The likelihood of such processes leading to a sense of the child having a belonging relationship with the school are almost nil.

Full-Service Schools: Links with Developmental Resources

One argument heard frequently in response to discussions of schools and high-risk students is that schools cannot do the job of the family. This would be an expected response to a couple of the parent needs listed earlier (Lein et al., 1992). How can schools provide support for parents to deal with discipline? or get their GED? or deal with substance-abuse problems in the home? These tasks are considered the province of other institutions, social service agencies, churches, or families themselves. But what happens when schools are the *only* organizing influence in a child's life? If schools are to be contexts for development then are they not responsible for playing a role in a relationship with the child's family? Is it possible to wait until society is restructured sufficiently to reduce the life hazards that families and children face? Probably not: Children and schools exist in the here and now.

Consistent with the idea that schooling is a context for development that involves an asymmetric relationship between mature and immature systems is that schools must be active in integrating themselves with other resources for development that exist within the community system (Holtzmann, 1992). Many of the reform efforts funded by the Hogg Foundation Initiative on the School of the Future (Holtzmann, 1992) reflect the premise that schools can be integrated with other resources for development and become places where these resources are channeled, funneled, focused, and at times delivered, in an effort to reduce risk. In this way, schools can counter overdifferentiation in systems involving families and other agencies.

In one example of such a full-service school implemented in Dallas, services offered in the school included before- and after-school care (offered by YMCA and YWCA); preventive interventions with behavior-disordered youth (Juvenile Justice); recreational activities (Boys' Club); job-training skills (Urban League); social services, such as Food Stamps (Human Service Department); and mental health and job training counseling (various agencies). Altman (1991) also argues that when services are linked in a particular context and become family centered (not agency centered), they are more functional and effective in supporting families.

Schools have a stake in supporting the development of families and children. Resources that exist in communities can be more focused and integrated (Schorr & Schorr, 1988). Schools are a logical and functional choice to be the site of this integration. Schools can assert themselves as leaders in communities in terms of creating contexts for the suitable development of children. This is not equivalent to saying that individual teachers, principals, or school counselors will provide job training or substance-abuse intervention, but that schools are a context in which families can come to be supported by these kinds of services—and schools provide these services indirectly when they make room for them in their buildings and in their procedures.

Slicing Time in Child-Supportive Ways

Schools and schooling carve up activity in many ways and along many dimensions. One crucial dimension is time. Overdifferentiation with respect to time occurs when there are too many time-coded boundaries in a child's school day or school career. The activities of a child during a day in school are dictated by schedules. The career of a child in the 13 or more years he or she spends in public schooling is marked by transitions coded to the number of years in school. Very large changes in how children are treated or viewed by schools (macro-regulations) are coded by time—entry to middle school, content-based curricula, and so on.

There is clearly a need for daily schedules and demarcations of school careers, but every time-coded transition is really a differentiation—a creation of a boundary—that the child must negotiate. Like boundaries between home and school, or between school and community agencies, these boundaries intensify risk when the linkages and interactions that enhance conversations across boundaries are not in place. Risk is intensified when, for example, the special-education resource program is not integrated with the mainstream curriculum, or when expectations in one setting do not correspond to those in another. Unlike the boundaries between home and school or school and agencies, time-coded boundaries are well within the control of the school, and are frequently arbitrary in relation to the child's development.

Consider the transitions schools create in the lives of children between the ages of 5 and 8. These children will have to form functional relationships with at least four different adult classroom teachers, and many more adults if teacher aides and adults linked to special services are involved. Frequently high-risk children are involved with the largest number of adults (teachers, aides, Chapter-1 teachers, speech services, special education). Under such conditions how do children come to have a sense that expectations are stable, that the tolerances built into social interactions are predictable? What structures are available to form and organize the child's development when instability is the rule?

Classroom routines for these children will change dramatically across their first four years in school and may well be driven more by when the art teacher is available than when the child can benefit from art activities. In one half-day prekindergarten classroom, one of us observed no fewer than 15 scheduled transitions each day. Consider the effect (on both children and teacher) of having to get 18 four-year-olds to stop an activity and reorient them to another one more than 15 times a day! Furthermore, when the child does not understand the nature of the transition or does not experience it as a function of her or his own behavior (that is, adult action is predicated on the child's behavior), then transitions are experienced as arbitrary, and the environment provides very little feedback function for the child. How does the teacher come to know the whole child, or school become knowable to children, under such circumstances?

Clearly, decreasing transition points, and making transitions less arbitrary, are two solutions to risk created by the problem of overdifferentiation of time. Unfortunately, most solutions to perceived problems in the schools only intensify risk by increasing transitions and making them more arbitrary. Recall the prekindergarten, high-risk girl we discussed in an earlier chapter who was playing in the house corner and narrating her play in complex language forms, and who was then interrupted by the speech pathologist who had an assignment to practice phonemes with the child.

Likewise, the transition points imposed on school careers can be equally arbitrary and risk-inducing and can be rethought in light of the problem of overdifferentiation of time. Educators tend to approach learning and behavior with short-term goals in mind—especially when seeking solutions to problems. Consider a longer, undifferentiated view of time, in which (when considering how to educate high-risk four-year-olds), schools ask the question "Where do we want these children to be (know, behave, etc.) when they are 16?" instead of "what do we need to teach these children this year (month, week), or how do we get these kids ready for next year?" Focusing on the short-term question, without strong attention to the more important long-term formulations, easily leads to disjointed programming and curricula, in which learning experiences are isolated from one another and from the broader context of the child's life.

Holistic Perspectives

In sum, we see overdifferentiation as a logical consequence of the reductionist mind-set permeating schooling for the past many decades. When faced with problems we have "looked downward" in the hierarchy of systems involved in the problem. When a child has difficulty learning to read, we measure lots of abilities we think are components of reading. When trying to offer assistance and support to children who might need it, we create new relationships and new time slots in the child's schedule. If a child's family has a problem we refer them, and the child, to an agency across town and forget about it—leaving the family and the problem to someone else. From the perspective of the Contextual Systems Model, when approaches are not well integrated into existing developmentally supportive structures, they make schooling more complex and less negotiable.

One solution, according to the Contextual Systems Model, is to "look-upward" through hierarchically arranged systems in a more holistic approach to problems. A holistic perspective addresses the "problem" from a wider angle and offers a new lens on solutions. The solution to wide ranges of individual variability in a classroom might be, for example, more generalists with higher levels of contact with children, and fewer specialists with little contact. Another might be looking at a child's experience of schooling as a whole in deciding how to schedule and structure that very lengthy journey. A third could involve seeing the school as a system with strong, identifiable links to family and community—a hub within a larger network of resources instead of a piece of a pie.

DEVELOPMENTALLY SUPPORTIVE SYSTEMS
Contextual Systems approaches to schooling and risk emphasize the interconnected nature of the child, home, school, community, and their components. Features often ascribed to children, such as risk or competence, are actually distributed across interconnected systems. A wide range of educational reform efforts fail in large part because they fail to ackowledge these facts.

A similar criticism can be made of the "Developmentally Appropriate Practices" (DAP) movement. As noted early in the book, much of the discourse on early school is now dominated by the notion of "developmentally appropriate practice" (DAP). In that discussion we called attention to the fact that DAP was viewed as the only discourse, and that it ignored several contemporary realities. Based as it is on a very individualized notion of development (Walsh, 1991), it is in its own way as reductionist as the practices it seeks to replace—development is reduced to a function of the individual organism. The emphasis on the role of environment masks the fact that the environment is defined very one dimensionally.

Reforms that focus solely on practice to ameliorate risk can also lead quickly to another form of reductionism, in which the larger frame of a problem is lost in a narrowly focused effort to solve it. Risk reduction in systems responsible for child development will not occur by changing individual activities that occur within that system or with the child, but with asking questions regarding the developmentally supportive qualities of the school as a mature system. DAP is an example of what happens when the answers to problems are decontextualized, when out-of-context solutions are viewed as "the" solutions. This problem is not unique to DAP. It occurs when school boards decide how to run classrooms, or when schools of education are viewed as the only means of generating new ideas about teaching. We argue that because schooling is embedded in complex local realities, the best solution that can be offered from the outside are solutions that encourage and support localities to solve their own problems. This is not a call for isolation, but a recognition that aside from generic principles, effective solutions in one place are not easily transplanted to another (Schorr et al., 1991).

Systems principles can be transplanted: for example, reduce overdifferentiation and increase integration, seek organization, create open systems and not closed systems by allowing new information in, enhance feedback loops, seek solutions at holistic levels. These principles can be applied to certain problems (as discussed above in terms of scheduling or with regard to add-on services in the schools), but the shape they take in particular places cannot be replicated. Similarly, individual practices cannot be judged without reference to the larger context in which they are implemented. In this way, we emphasize that the unit that is developmentally supportive is a system, not a practice.

Schooling As Conversation

Schooling can be profitably seen as conversation. Three ideas drawn from the work of Margaret Donaldson provide a place from which to begin to understand the child's difficulty in entering into that conversation. First, the child brings to school his or her "human sense," that is, the understanding she or he has constructed of the world through her or his efforts to make sense of actions and interactions. Bruner (1990a) synopsized Donaldson's (1978) thinking this way: "local knowledge, related to particular situations, always precedes general knowledge" (p. x). To some extent that human sense is always idiosyncratic, and often it remains hidden from the adult who does not attend closely. Second, we need to consider the situations in which children find themselves, or as is more often the case, into which we put them, from the children's point of view, something we seldom do, and as Donaldson shows, Piagetian theory is particularly derelict in doing. And finally, we need to constantly remind ourselves of both the importance and difficulty of formal education for the young child, for all young children, and particularly for those most likely to be dubbed high risk (Grieve & Hughes, 1990).

If schools are to engage children meaningfully in conversation, we are going to have to attend carefully the understanding of the world they bring with them to school, we are going to have to be able to take their perspective, we are going to have take seriously the difficult challenge that formal learning presents all children, but the bottom third in particular. And finally we are going to have to not back away from the importance of formal schooling. As we said at the beginning, schools are going to have to have to become more intellectually demanding, especially for the bottom third.

CONCLUSIONS

Changes that flow from the Contextual Systems Model are subtle, not easily measured, observed, or transferred from classroom to classroom, school to school, or family to family. In the largest sense, CSM advocates changes that accomplish two things: (1) increasing knowledge about the lives of children who come to school, and (2) creating open, flexible, integrated whole systems that wrap children and sustain them.

Schools need to know a lot about the children who attend. Schools need to know the meaning that children make of their experiences there, not so much whether a particular kids' parents are divorcing or not. This information may be useful but not on its own. Instead it is more important to know how this experience affects the child's understanding of school. Then resources can be delivered to sustain this child. Knowledge and the desire to understand are the key integrative links across systems that will enhance their capacity to support development. When parents ask what their child is doing in school or when teachers want to know how they can best approach a child, they are asking about information available to another system that is not available to them. Increasing information flow of this sort is crucial to development for all children, but particularly for high-risk children.

Our second point is related to the first. Information does not flow easily in closed, overdifferentiated systems. Can we evaluate schools in terms of the quality and quantity of feedback loops present in its operation—between teacher and children, parents and teachers, teachers and principals, even between children and principals, and so on? Can the constraints built into these systems—artificial boundaries between developmentally sustaining resources, negative biases, lack of interaction—be reduced in an effort to increase openness?

Finally, information abut contemporary realities is very important for schools. We started this book by describing the grim realities faced by children growing up in America in the last decade of the 20th century. Schools will only be supportive places for child development if they attend to this information and take it to heart, not to try to change all the conditions that give rise to these realities, but to use this information to understand the contexts in which children are developing, and consequently, the level of support they will need when they attend school. Pretending these realities will someday go away, and pretending that education will play a part in these realities going away, without acknowledging that these risks are real and require attention, is to collude in a tragedy.

These harsh realities are overrepresented in certain sectors of American culture, correlated with race, ethnicity, and income. Risk is not random; it is predictable, and highly predictable in some forms. What Kozol (1991) called "savage inequalities" pervade our culture. The fact that some children escape the ravages of risk in these circumstances should not deflect attention from the large number of children who do not escape, and for whom school is not a means of reducing risk exposure. Multicultural perspectives cannot mute the harshness of reality for the children who live in these circumstances, but schools can.

It all comes down to a question of attitude. Theory confers on the reader a view of reality, a window on the world, a way of understanding contemporary reality that leads to action. We hope that the theory we present offers a way of seeing children and the problems associated with their education that leads educators, all of us, to seeing these children and their problems in a very different way from how we have been seeing them. Ultimately, we need to reframe the questions that are asked about high-risk children. We need to move from questions that cannot be answered or cannot be answered in ways that support a child's development to questions that can be answered in developmentally supportive ways.

References

Aber, J. L., & Allen, J. P. (1987). The effects of maltreatment on young children's socioemotional development: An attachment perspective. *Developmental Psychology, 23,* 406–414.

Ainsworth, M. D., Blehar, M. C., Waters, E., & Wall, D. (1978). *Patterns of attachment: A psychological study of the strange situation.* Hillsdale, NJ: Erlbaum.

Alexander, K. L., & Entwisle, D. R. (1988). Achievement in the first two years of school: Patterns and processes. *Monographs of the Society for Research in Child Development, 53* (20, serial No. 218).

Algozzine, B., Christenson, S., & Ysseldyke, J. (1988). Probabilities associated with the referral-to-placement process. *Teacher Education and Special Education, 5,* 19–23.

Altman, D. (1991). The challenges of services integration for children and families. In L. B. Schorr, D. Both, & C. Copple (Eds.), *Effective services for young children: Report of a workshop* (pp. 74–79). Washington, DC: National Academy.

Apple, M. W. (1986). *Teachers and texts: A political economy of class and gender relations in education.* New York: Routledge and Kegan Paul.

————, & Weis, L. (Eds.) (1983). *Ideology and practice in education: A political and conceptual introduction.* Philadelphia: Temple University Press.

Asher, C. (1994). Retravelling the choice road. *Harvard Educational Review, 64,* 209–221.

Au, K. H. (1979). Using the experience-text-relationship method with minority children. *Reading Teacher, 32,* 677–679.

————. (1980). Participation structures in reading lessons with Hawaiian children. *Anthropology and Education Quarterly, 11,* 91–115.

————, & Jordan, C. (1981). Teaching reading to Hawaiian children: Finding a culturally appropriate solution. In H. Trueba, G. P. Guthrie, & D. H. Au (Eds.), *Culture and the bilingual classroom: Studies in classroom ethnography* (pp. 139–152). Rowley, MA: Newbury House.

Ayers, W. (1989). *The good preschool teacher: Six teachers reflect on their lives.* New York: Teachers College Press.

Ball, R., & Pianta, R. C. (1993). Maternal social support as a predictor of parental competence. *Early Development and Parenting, 2,* 209–216.

Bassuk, E. L. (1989). Homelessness: A growing American tragedy. *Division of Child, Youth, and Family Services Newsletter, 12*(4), 1,13.

Beeghly, M., & Cicchetti, D. (1994). Child maltreatment, attachment, and the self system: Emergence of an internal state lexicon in toddlers at high social risk. *Development and Psychopathology, 6*, 5–30.

Belle, D. (1982). The stress of caring: Women as providers of social support. In L. Goldberger & S. Breznitz (Eds.), *The handbook of stress* (pp. 496–505). New York: Free Press.

Belsky, J. (1984). The determinants of parenting: A process model. *Child Development, 55*, 83–96.

Bereiter, C., & Engelmann, S. (1966). *Teaching disadvantaged children in the preschool.* Englewood Cliffs, NJ: Prentice Hall.

Borkowski, J. G., & Dukewich, T. L. (in press). Environmental covariations and intelligence: How attachement influences self-regulation. In D. Detterman (Ed.), *Current topics in human intelligence.* Norwood, NJ: Ablex.

Bornstein, M. H. (1989). Sensitive periods in development: Structural characteristics and causal interpretations. *Psychological Bulletin, 105*, 179–197.

Boulding, K. E. (1985). *The world as total system.* Beverly Hills, CA: Sage.

Bourdieu, P., & Passeron, C. (1977). *Reproduction in education, society and culture.* Los Angeles: Sage.

Bowlby, J. (1969). *Attachment and loss, vol. 1: Attachment.* New York: Basic Books.

Bowles, S., & Gintis, H. I. (1976). *Schooling in capitalist America.* New York: Basic Books.

Boyer, E. (1983). *High school: A report on secondary education in America.* New York: Harper and Row.

Bracey, G. W. (1991, October). Why can't they be like we were? *Phi Delta Kappan*, pp. 104–117.

———. (1992, October). The second Bracey report on the condition of public education, *Phi Delta Kappan*, pp. 104–117.

Bradley, R. H., & Caldwell, B. M.(1976). Early home environment and changes in mental test performance in children from 6 to 36 months. *Developmental Psychology, 12*, 93–97.

———, & Rock, S. L. (1988). Home environment and school performance: A ten year follow up and examination of three models of environmental action. *Child Development, 59*, 852–867.

Bredekamp, S. (1987). *Developmentally appropriate practice in early childhood programs serving children from birth through age 8.* Washington, DC: National Association for the Education of Young Children.

Bronfenbrenner, U. (1979). *The ecology of human development: Experiments by nature and design.* Cambridge, MA: Harvard University Press.

———. (1986). Ecology of the family as a context for human development: Research perspective. *Developmental Psychology, 32*, 513–531.

Brown, R. (1991). *Schools of thought.* San Francisco: Jossey-Bass.

Bruner, J. S. (1966). *Towards a theory of instruction.* Cambridge, MA: Harvard University Press.

————. (1987). The transactional self. In J. S. Bruner & H. Haste (Eds.), *Making sense: The child's construction of the world* (pp. 81–96). London: Methuen.

————. (1990a). Foreward. In R. Grieve & M. Hughes (Eds.), *Understanding children: Essays in honor of Margaret Donaldson* (pp. vii–xii). London: Basil Blackwell.

————. (1990b). *Acts of meaning.* Cambridge, MA: Harvard University Press.

————, & Haste, H. (1987). *Making sense: The child's construction of the world.* London: Methuen.

Bus, A. G, & van IZjendoorn, M. H. (1988). Mother-child interactions, attachment, and emergent literacy: A cross-sectional study. *Child Development, 59,* 1262–1273.

Callahan, R. (1962). *Education and the cult of efficiency.* Chicago: University of Chicago Press.

Cameron, S., & Heckman, J. (1993). Nonequivalence of high school equivalents. *Journal of Labor Economics, 11*(1), 1–47.

Canam, C. (1986). Perceived stressors and coping responses of employed and non-employed career women with preschool children. *Canadian Journal of Community Health, 5,* 49–59.

Cassidy, J. (1994). Emotion regulation: Influences of attachment relationships. In N. A. Fox (Ed.), *The development of emotion regulation: Biological and behavioral considerations. Monographs of the Society for Research in Child Development, 59* (Serial No. 240), 228–249.

Ceglowski, D. (1995). *Policies from practice: The story of the Whitewater Headstart.* Unpublished doctoral dissertation, University of Illinois at Urbana-Champaign.

Chubb, J. E., & Moe, T. M. (1990). *Politics, markets and American schools.* Washington, DC: Brooking Institution.

Cicchetti, D. (1994). Advances and challenges in the study of the sequelae of child maltreatment. *Development and Psychopathology, 6,* 1–4.

————, & Tucker, D. (1994). Development and self-regulatory structures of the mind. *Development and Psychopathology, 6,* 533–550.

Clark, D. L., & Astuto, T. A. (1988). *Education policy after Reagan: What next.* Charlottesville, VA: Policy Studies Center of the University Council for Educational Administration.

Cohn, J., Campbell, S., Matias, R., & Hopkins, J. (1990). Face-to-face interactions of postpartum depressed and non-depressed mother-infant pairs. *Developmental Psychology, 26,* 15–23.

Comer, J. P. (1980). *School power.* New York: Free Press.

———. (1985). The Yale-New Haven Primary Prevention Project: A follow-up study. *Journal of the American Academy of Child Psychiatry, 24*(2), 154–160.

———. (1988). Educating poor minority children. *Scientific American, 259*(5); 42–48.

Conduct Problems Prevention Research Group. (1992). A developmental and clinical model for the prevention of conduct disorder: The FAST track program. *Development and Psychopathology, 4,* 509–528.

Connell, R. W. (1994). Poverty and education. *Harvard Educational Review, 64,* 125–149.

Cowen, E. L. (1980). The Primary Mental Health Project: Yesterday, today, and tomorrow. *Journal of Special Education, 14,* 133–154.

Crittenden, P. M. (1992). Quality of attachment in the preschool years. *Development and Psychopathology, 4,* 209–242.

Crnic, K., Greenberg, M., Ragozin, A., Robinson, N., & Basham, R. (1983). Effects of stress and social support on mothers and premature and full term infants. *Child Development, 54,* 209–217.

Crockenberg, S. (1981) Infant irritability, mother responsiveness, and social support influences on the security of infant-mother attachment. *Child Development, 52,* 857–865.

Cronbach, L. J. (1975). Beyond the two disciplines of scientific inquiry. *American Psychologist, 30,* 116–127.

Cuban, L. (1976). *Urban school chiefs under fire.* Chicago: University of Chicago Press.

———. (1989, June). The "at-risk" label and the problem of urban school reform. *Phi Delta Kappan,* pp. 780–784, 789–801.

———. (1994, June 15). The great school scam: The economy's turned around, but where is the praise? *Education Week,* p. 44.

Cummings, E. M., Hennessy, K., Rabideau, G., & Cicchetti, D. (1994). Responses of physically abused boys to interadult anger involving their mothers. *Development and Psychopathology, 6,* 31–42.

Cziko, G. A. (1992). Purposeful behavior as the control of perception: Implications for educational research. *Educational Researcher, 21*(9), 10–18, 27.

D'Amato, J. (1988). "Acting": Hawaiian children's resistance to teachers. *Elementary School Journal, 88,* 529–544.

DeMulder, E., & Radke-Yarrow, M. (1991). Attachment with affectively ill and well mothers: Concurrent behavioral correlates. *Development and Psychopathology, 3,* 227–242.

Dodge, K., Pettit, G., & Bates, J. (1994). Effects of maltreatment on the development of peer relations. *Development and Psychopathology, 6,* 43–57.

Donaldson, M. (1978). *Children's minds.* New York: W. W. Norton.

Doyle, W., & Ponder, G. A. (1977–1978). The practicality ethic in teacher decision making. *Interchange, 8,* 1–12.

Duncan, G. J. (1991). The economic environment of childhood. In A.C. Huston (Ed.), *Children in poverty: Child development and public policy* (pp. 23–50). New York: Cambridge University Press.

———. (1993, March). *Gender differences in the effects of family and neighborhoods on completed schooling.* Paper presented at the Biannual Meeting of the Society for Research in Child Development, New Orleans, LA.

Durkin, D. (1987, April). Testing in kindergarten. *Reading Teacher,* pp. 766–770.

Eaton, W. (1981). Demographic and social-ecologic risk factors for mental disorders. In D. Regier & A. Gordon (Eds.), *Risk factor research in the major mental disorders* (pp. 111–130). Washington, DC: U.S. Government Printing Office.

Editors of *Education Week* (1993). *From risk to renewal: Charting a course for reform.* Washington, DC: Editorial Projects in Education.

Ekstrom, R. B., Goertz, M. E., Pollack, J. M., & Rock, D. A. (1986). Who drops out of high school and why? Findings from a national study. *Teachers College Record, 87,* 356–373.

Ellwein, M. C., & Glass, G. V. (1989). Ending social promotion in Waterford: Appearances and reality. In L. A. Shepard & M. L. Smith (Eds.), *Flunking grades: Research and policies on retention* (pp. 151–173). New York: Falmer Press.

———, Walsh, D. J., Eads, G. M., & Miller, A. K. (1991). Using readiness tests to route kindergarten students: The snarled intersection of psychometrics, policy, and practice. *Educational Evaluation and Policy Analysis, 13,* 159–175.

Emery, R. (1982). Interparental conflict and the children of divorce. *Psychological Bulletin, 92,* 310–330.

Entwistle, D. R., & Alexander, K. L. (1993, March). *How neighborhood resources produce gender differences in the math competence of 6 to 8 year old children.* Paper presented at the Biannual Meeting of the Society for Research in Child Development, New Orleans, LA.

Erickson, E. (1968). *Children and society.* New York: Norton.

Erickson, F. (1992, April). *Post-everything: The word of the moment and how we got here.* Paper presented at the Annual Meeting of the American Educational Research Association, San Francisco, CA.

Erickson, M. F., Egeland, B., & Pianta, R. C. (1989). The effects of maltreatment on the development of young children. In D. Cicchetti & V. Carlson (Eds.), *Child maltreatment: Theory and research on the causes and conse-*

quences of child abuse and neglect (pp. 647–684). New York: Cambridge University Press.

Erickson, M. F., Sroufe, L. A., & Egeland, B. (1985). The relationship between quality of attachment and behavior problems in preschool in a high-risk sample. In I. Bretherton & E. Waters (Eds.), *Growing points of attachment: Theory and research. Monographs for the Society of Research in Child Development, vol. 50, nos. 1–2* (serial no. 209). Chicago: University of Chicago Press.

Field, T. (1989). Maternal depression effects on infant interaction and attachment behavior. In D. Cicchetti & S. Toth (Eds.). *Rochester Symposium on Developmental Psychopathology, vol. 1: The Emergence of a Discipline* (pp. 139–164). Hillsdale, NJ: Erlbaum.

Fine, M. (1986). Why urban adolescents drop into and out of public high school. *Teachers College Record, 87,* 393–409.

———. (1991). *Framing dropouts: Notes on the politics of an urban public high school.* Albany, NY: SUNY.

———, & Rosenberg, P. (1983). Dropping out of high school: The ideology of school and work. *Journal of Education, 165,* 257–272.

Fonagy, P., Steele, H., & Steele, M. (1991). Maternal representations of attachment during pregnancy predict the organization of mother-infant attachment at one year of age. *Child Development, 62,* 891–905.

Ford, D. H, & Ford, M. E. (1987). *Humans as self-constructing living systems.* Hillsdale, NJ: Erlbaum.

———, & Lerner, R. M. (1992). *Developmental systems theory: An integrative approach.* Newbury Park, CA: Sage.

Fordham Institute for Innovation in Social Policy. (1992). *Index of social health.* Author.

Garbarino, J. (1982). *Children and families in the social environment.* New York: Aldine.

———, Dubrow, N., Kostelny, K., & Pardo, C. (1992). *Children in danger: Coping with the consequences of community violence.* San Francisco: Jossey-Bass.

———, & Sherman, D. (1980). High-risk neighborhoods and high-risk families: The human ecology of child maltreatment. *Child Development, 51,* 188–198.

———, & Vondra, J. (1987). Psychological maltreatment: Issues and perspectives. In M. R. Brassard, R. Germain, & S. Hart (Eds.), *Psychological maltreatment of children and youth* (pp. 254–266). New York: Pergammon.

Garmezy, N. (1977). On some risks in risk research. *Psychological Medicine, 7,* 1–6.

————. (1984). Stress-resistant children: The search for protective factors. In J. E. Stevenson (Ed.), *Aspects of current child psychiatry research.* Oxford: Pergammon Press.

Gartner, A., & Lipsky, K. K. (1987). Beyond special education: Toward a quality system for all students. *Harvard Educational Review, 57,* 368–395.

Gaskins, S., Miller, P. J., & Corsaro, W. A. (1992). Theoretical and methodological perspectives in the interpretive study of children. In W. A. Corsaro & P. J. Miller (Eds.), *Interpretive approaches to children's socialization* (pp. 5–23). San Francisco: Jossey-Bass.

Gelman, R. (1979). Preschool thought. *American Psychologist, 34,* 900–905.

————, & Baillargeon, R. (1983). A review of some Piagetian concepts. In P. H. Mussen (Ed.), *Handbook of child psychology, volume III, cognitive development* (J. Flavell & E. M. Markham, volume editors, pp. 167–230). New York: Wiley.

Glasser, W. (1993). *The quality school teacher.* New York: Harper-Collins.

Goodlad, J. I. (1983a). Access to knowledge. *Teachers College Record, 84,* 787–800.

————. (1983b). The school as workplace. In G. A.Griffin (Ed.), *Staff development, Eighty-second yearbook of the National Society for the Study of Education* (pp. 36–61). Chicago: University of Chicago Press.

Gormoran, A. (1987, July). The stratification of high school learning opportunities. *Sociology of Education, 60,* 135–155.

Gottlieb, G. (1991). Experimental canalization of behavioral development: Theory. *Developmental Psychology, 27,* 4–13.

Gould, S. J. (1981). *The mismeasure of man.* New York: W. W. Norton.

Graue, M. E. (1993). *Ready for what? Constructing meanings of readiness for kindergarten.* Albany, NY: SUNY.

————, & Walsh, D. J. (1995). Children in context: Interpreting the here and now of children's lives. In A. Hatch (Ed.), *Qualitative research in early childhood settings* (pp. 135–154). Westport, CT: Greenwood Press.

Greenberg, M. T., Cicchetti, D., & Cummings, M. (1990). *Attachment in the preschool years.* Chicago: University of Chicago Press.

————, Kusche, C. A., & Speltz, M. (1990). Emotional regulation, self-control, and psychopathology: The role of relationships in early childhood. In D. Cicchetti & S. Toth (Eds.), *Rochester Symposium on Developmental Psychopathology, vol. 2, Internalizing and Enternalizing Expressions of Dysfunction* (pp. 21–55). Hillsdale, NJ: Erlbaum.

Greenough, W. T., & Black, J. E. (1991). Induction of brain structure by experience: Substrates for cognitive development. In M. Gunnar & C. A. Nelson (Eds.), *Behavioral developmental neuroscience: Vol. 24. Minnesota symposia on child psychology* (pp. 155–200). Hillsdale, NJ: Erlbaum.

Greenspan, S. I. (1989). *Development of the ego.* Madison, CT: International Universities Press.

———, & Greenspan, N. (1991). *Clinical interview of the child* (2nd. ed.). Madison, CT: International Universities Press.

———. & Porges, S. W. (1984). Psychopathology in infancy and early childhood: Clinical perspectives on the organization of sensory and affective-thematic experience. *Child Development, 55,* 49–70.

Greenstein, R. (1992, September). *Analysis of poverty in 1991.* Washington, DC: Center on Budget and Policy Priorities.

Grieve, R., & Hughes, M. (1990), *Understanding children: Essays in honor of Margaret Donaldson.* Cambridge, MA: Basil Blackwell.

Gross, N. (1958). *Who runs our schools?* New York: Wiley.

Haller, E. J. (1985). Pupil race and elementary school ability grouping: Are teachers biased against black children? *American Educational Research Journal, 22,* 465–483.

Harp, B. (1993). *Bringing children to literacy: Classroom at work.* Norwood, MA: Christopher-Gordon.

Heath, S. B. (1983). *Ways with words: Language, life, and work in communities and classrooms.* Cambridge: Cambridge University Press.

Hennessy, K. D., Rabideau, G. J., Cicchetti, D., & Cummings, E. M. (1994). Responses of physically abused and nonabused children to different forms of interadult anger. *Child Development, 65,* 815–828.

Herbst, J. (1989). *And sadly teach: Teacher education and professionalization in American culture.* Madison, WI: University of Wisconsin.

Hess, G. A., Wells, E., Prindle, C., Lippman, P., & Kaplan, B. (1987). Where's room 185? How schools can reduce their dropout problem. *Education and Urban Society, 19,* 330–355.

Hetherington, E.M. (1989). Coping with family transitions: Winners, losers and survivors. *Child Development, 60,* 1–14.

Hinde, R. (1987). *Individuals, relationships, and culture.* New York: Cambridge University Press.

Hofer, M. A. (1994). Hidden regulators in attachment, separation, and loss. In N. A. Fox (Ed.), *The development of emotion regulation: Biological and behavioral considerations. Monographs of the Society for Research in Child Development, 59* (Serial No. 240), pp. 192–207.

Holmes, C. T. (1989). Grade level retention effects: A meta-analysis of research studies. In L. A. Shepard & M. L. Smith (Eds.), *Flunking grades: Research and policies on retention* (pp. 16–33). New York: Falmer Press.

———, & Matthews, K. M. (1984). The effects of nonpromotion on elementary and junior high school pupils: A meta-analysis. *Review of Educational Research, 54,* 225–236.

Holtzman, W. H. (1992). *School of the future.* Washington, DC: American Psychological Association.

Howes, C., & Hamilton, C. E. (1992). Children's relationships with child care teachers: Stability and concordance with parental attachments. *Child Development, 63,* 867–878.

Huston, A.C. (1991). Children in poverty: Developmental and policy issues. In A.C. Huston (Ed.), *Children in poverty: Child development and public policy* (pp. 1–22). New York: Cambridge University Press.

Inagaki, K. (1992). Piagetian and post-Piagetian conceptions of development and their implications for science education in early childhood. *Early Childhood Research Quarterly, 7,* 115–133.

Institute for Educational Leadership (1986). *School boards: Strengthening grass roots leadership.* Washington, DC: Author.

Jackson, G. B. (1975). The research evidence on the effects of grade retention. *Review of Educational Research, 45,* 613–635.

Jackson, P. W. (1968). *Life in classrooms.* New York: Holt, Rinehart & Winston.

Jencks, C. (1988, June 13). Deadly neighborhoods. *New Republic,* pp. 23–32.

Jones, J. E. (1994). *Child poverty: A deficit that goes beyond dollars.* New York: National Center for Children in Poverty.

Kaus, M. (1992). *The end of equality.* New York: Basic Books.

Keating, D. P. (in press). Habits of mind: Developmental diversity in competence and coping. In D. K. Detterman (ed.), *Current topics in human intelligence.* Norwood, NJ: Ablex.

Kessler, S., & Swadener, B. B. (1992). *Reconceptualizing the early childhood curriculum: Beginning the dialogue.* New York: Teachers College Press.

Kozol, J. (1991). *Savage inequalities: Children in American schools.* New York: Crown.

Ladd, G. W., Price, J. M., & Hart, C. H. (1988). Predicting preschoolers' peer status from their playground behaviors. *Child Development, 59,* 986–992.

Lawton, J. T., & Hooper, F. H. (1978). Piagetian theory and early childhood education: A critical analysis. In C. Brainerd & L. Siegel (Eds.), *Alternatives to Piaget: Critical essays on the theory* (pp. 169–199). New York: Academic Press.

Lazar, I., Darlington, R., Murray, H., Royce, J., & Snipper, A. (1982). Lasting effects of early education: A report for the Consortium for Longitudinal Studies. *Monographs of the Society for Research in Child Development, 47* (2–3, Serial No. 194).

Lee, J. (1995). *In between worlds: Being a lab school teacher.* Unpublished doctoral dissertation, University of Illinois at Urbana-Champaign.

Lewis, C. (1995). *Educating hearts and minds: Reflection on Japanese preschool and elementary education.* Cambridge: Cambridge University Press.

Lein, L., Radle, P., & Radle, R. (1992). San Antonio Family Support Program: Reflections on the school of the future in the center of a public housing project. In W. H. Holtzman (Ed.), *School of the future* (pp. 85–96). Washington, DC: American Psychological Association.

Li, J., & Bennett, N. (1994). *Young children in poverty: A statistical update.* New York: National Center for Children in Poverty.

Lieberman, A. F. (1992). Infant-parent psychotherapy with toddlers. *Development and Psychopathology, 4,* 559–574.

Lyons-Ruth, K. (1992). Maternal depressive symptoms, disorganized infant-mother attachment relationships and hostile-aggressive behavior in the preschool classroom: A prospective longitudinal view from infancy to age five. In D. Cicchetti & S. Toth (Eds.). *Rochester symposium on developmental psychopathology, vol. 4: Developmental perspectives on depression* (pp. 131–172). Rochester, NY: University of Rochester Press.

McLanahan, S. S, Astone, N. M., & Marks, N. F. (1991). The role of mother-only families in reproducing poverty. In A. C. Huston (Ed.), *Children in poverty: Child development and public policy* (pp. 51–78). New York: Cambridge University Press.

McLoyd, V., Javartne, T., Ceballo, R., & Borquez, J. (1994). Unemployment and work interruption among African American single mothers: Effects on parenting and adolescent socioemotional functioning. *Child Development, 65,* 562–589.

McLoyd, V. C., & Wilson, L. (1991). The strain of living poor: Parenting, social support, and child mental health. In A. C. Huston (Ed.), *Children in poverty: Child development and public policy* (pp. 105–135). New York: Cambridge.

Maeroff, G. I. (1988, May). Withered hopes, still born dreams: The dismal panorama of urban schools. *Phi Delta Kappan,* pp. 633–638.

Main, M., & Hesse E. (1990). Is fear the link between infant disorganized attachment status and maternal unresolved loss? In M. Greenberg, D. Cicchetti, & M. Cummings (Eds.), *Attachment in the preschool years* (pp. 161–182). Chicago: University of Chicago Press.

Margolis, L. (1982). Help wanted. *Pediatrics, 69,* 816–818.

Martin, R. P. (1988). *Assessment of personality and behavior problems: Infancy through adolescence.* New York: Guilford.

Masten, A. S. (1992). Homeless children in the United States: Mark of a nation at risk. *Current Directions in Psychological Science, 1,* 41–44.

Mattson (1993). *Factbook on elementary, middle, and secondary schools: 1993.* New York: Scholastic.

Meisels, S. J. (1987). Uses and abuses of developmental screening and school readiness testing. *Young Children, 42*(2), 4–9.

Moynihan, D. P. (1993). Defining deviancy down. *American Scholar, 62,* 17–30.

Munroe, B. M., Boyle, M. H., & Offord, D. R. (1988). Single parent families: Child psychiatric disorder and school performance. *Journal of the American Academy of Child and Adolescent Psychiatry, 27,* 214–219.

National Center for Children in Poverty. (1993). *Five million children: 1993 update.* New York: Author.

National Center for Health Statistics. (1993). *Children's health index.* Hyattsville, MD: Public Health Service.

National Research Council. (1990). *Who cares for America's children?* Washington, DC: National Academy of Sciences.

Natriello, G. (1986). School dropouts: Patterns and policies. *Teachers College Record, 87,* 305–306.

———, & Dornbusch, S. M. (1983). Bringing behavior back in: The effects of student characteristics and behaviors on the classroom behavior of teachers. *American Educational Research Journal, 20,* 1, 29–43.

———, Pallas, A. M., McDill, E. L., McPartland, J. M., & Royster, D. (1988). *An examination of the assumptions and evidence for alternative dropout prevention programs in high schools.* Baltimore, MD: Center for Social Organization of Schools.

Ogbu, J. (1974). *The next generation: An ethnography of education in an urban neighborhood.* New York: Academic Press.

———. (1981). Origins of human competence: A cultural-ecological perspective. *Child Development, 52,* 413–429.

———. (1982). Socialization: A cultural ecological approach. In K. M. Borman (Ed.), *The social life of children in a changing society.* (pp. 253–267). Hillsdale, NJ: Erlbaum.

Olson, L., & Bradley, A. (1992, April 29). Boards of contention. *Eduction Week Special Report,* pp. 1–11.

Parker, J. G., & Asher, S. R. (1987). Peer relations and later peer adjustment: Are lower-accepted children "at-risk"? *Psychological Bulletin, 102,* 357–389.

Pederson, E., Faucher, T. A., & Eaton, W. W. (1978). A new perspective on the effects of first grade teachers on children's subsequent adult status. *Harvard Educational Review, 48,* 1–31.

Pennington, B. F., & Ozonoff, S. (1991). A neurological perspective on continuity and discontinuity in developmental psychopathology. In D. Cicchetti & S. L. Toth (Eds.), *Rochester Symposium on Developmental Psychopathology, vol. 3: Models and integrations* (pp. 117–160). Rochester, NY: University of Rochester Press.

Piaget, J. (1970). Piaget's theory. In P. H. Mussen (Ed.), *Carmichael's manual of child psychology, third edition* (pp. 703–722). New York: Wiley.

Pianta, R. C. (1990). Widening the debate on educational reform: Prevention as a viable alternative. *Exceptional Children, 56*, 306–313.

———. (1992). *Beyond the parent: The role of other adults in children's lives. New Directions in Child Development, vol. 57.* San Francisco: Jossey Bass.

———. (1994). Patterns of relationships between children and kindergarten teachers. *Journal of School Psychology, 32*, 15–32.

———, & Ball, R. (1993). Maternal social support as a predictor of adjustment in kindergarten. *Journal of Applied Developmental Psychology, 14*, 107–128.

———, & Egeland, B. (1995). *Findings from the Minnesota Mother-Child Project.* Unpublished manuscript.

———, Egeland, B., & Hyatt, A. (1986). Maternal relationship history as an indicator of developmental risk. *American Journal of Orthopsychiatry, 56*, 385–398.

———, Egeland, B., & Sroufe, L.A. (1990). Maternal stress and children's development: Prediction of school outcomes and identification of protective factors. In J. Rolf, A. Masten, D. Cicchetti, K. Nuechterlein, & S. Weintraub (Eds.), *Risk and protective factors in the development of psychopathology* (pp. 215–235). New York: Cambridge University Press.

———, & Nimetz, S. L. (1989). Educators' beliefs about risk and prevention: The context for changing beliefs. *Early Education and Development, 1*, 115–126.

———, Steinberg, M., & Rollins, K. (1995). The first two years of school: Teacher child relationships and deflections in children's classroom adjustment. *Development and Psychopathology, 7*, 297–312.

Public Health Service. (1992). *Health, United States 1992.* Washington, DC: Author.

Purkey, S. C., & Smith, M. S. (1983). Effective schools: A review. *Elementary School Journal, 83*, 427–452.

———. (1985). School reform: The district implications of the effective schools literature. *Elementary School Journal, 85*, 281–317.

Ramey, C. T., & Campbell, F. A. (1991). Poverty, early childhood education, and academic competence: The Abecedarian experiment. In A. C. Huston (Ed.), *Children in poverty: Child development and public policy* (pp. 190–221). New York: Cambridge University Press.

Reed, S., & Sautter, R. C. (1990, June). Children of poverty: The status of 12 million young Americans. *Phi Delta Kappan*, pp. 1–12.

Reeves, M. S. (1988, April 27). Self interest and the common weal: Focusing on the bottom half. *Education Week*, 14–21.

Reid, J. (1994). Prevention of conduct problems before and after school entry: Relating interventions to developmental findings. *Development and Psychopathology, 5*, 243–262.

Resnick, D. P., & Resnick, L. B. (1985). Standards, curriculum, and performance: A historical and comparative perspective. *Educational Researcher, 14*, 4, 5–20.

Resnick, L. B. (1991). Shared cognition: Thinking as social practice. In L. B. Resnick, J. M. Levine, & S. D. Teasely (Eds.), *Perspectives on socially shared cognition* (pp. 1–20). Washington, DC: American Psychological Association.

———. (1994). Situated rationalism: Biological and social preparation for learning. In L. Hirschfield & S. Gelman (Eds.), *Mapping the mind: Domain specificity in cognition and culture* (pp. 474–493). Cambridge, UK: Cambridge University Press.

———. (1995). Inventing arithmetic: Making children's intuition work in school (pp. 75–101). In C. A. Nelson (Ed.) *Basic and applied perspectives on learning, cognition, and development*, Hillsdale, NJ: Erlbaum.

Riccio, C. A., Hynd, G. W., Cohen, M. J., & Gonzalez, J. J. (1993). Neurological basis of attention deficit hyperactivity disorder. *Exceptional Children, 60*, 118–124.

Richardson-Koehler, V. (1988, April). *Teachers' beliefs about at-risk students.* Paper presented at the Annual Meeting of the American Educational Research Association, New Orleans, LA.

Rieff, D. (1991). *Los Angeles: Capital of the third world.* New York: Simon & Schuster.

Rogoff, B. (1990). *Apprenticeship in thinking: Cognitive development in social context.* New York: Oxford.

Romberg, T. A., & Price, G. G. (1983). Curriculum implementation and staff development as cultural change. In G. A. Griffin (Ed.), *Staff development: Eighty-second yearbook of the National Society for the Study of Education* (pp. 154–184). Chicago: University of Chicago Press.

Rosaldo, M. (1984). Toward an anthropology of self and feeling. In R. Schweder & R. LeVine (Eds.), *Culture theory: Essays on mind, self and emotion* (pp. 137–157). Cambridge: Cambridge University Press.

Rowan, B., & Denk, C. E. (1984). Management succession, school socioeconomic context, and basic skills achievement. *American Educational Research Journal, 21*, 517–537.

Rubin, K., Both, L., Zahn-Waxler, C., Cummings, E. M., & Wilkinson, M. (1991). Dyadic play behaviors of children of well and depressed mothers. *Development and Psychopathology, 3*, 243–252.

Rumberger, R. W. (1983). Dropping out of high school: The influence of race, sex, and family background. *American Educational Research Journal, 20*, 199–220.

Rutter, M. (1979). Protective factors in children's responses to stress and disadvantage. In M. W. Kent & J. E. Rolf (Eds.), *Primary prevention of psychopathology: Social competence in children* (pp. 49–74). Hanover, NH: University of New England Press.

———. (1987). Psychosocial resilience and protective mechanisms. *American Journal of Orthopsychiatry, 57*, 316–331.

Sameroff, A. J. (1983). Developmental systems: Context and evolution. In P. Mussen (Ed.), *Handbook of child psychology: Vol. 1, History, theory and methods* (pp. 237–294). New York: Wiley.

———. (1989). Principles of development and psychopathology. In A. Sameroff & R. Emde (Eds.), *Relationship disturbances in early childhood* (pp. 17–32). New York: Basic Books.

———, & Chandler, M. (1975). Reproductive risk and the continuum of caretaking casualty. In F. Horowitz, E. M. Hetherington, S. Scarr-Salapatek, & G. Siegel (Eds.), *Review of child development research, vol. 4* (pp.187–244). Chicago: University of Chicago.

———, & Emde, R. N. (1989). *Relationship disturbances in early childhood: A developmental approach.* New York: Basic Books.

———, & Seifer, R. (1984). Familial risk and child competence. *Child Development, 54*, 1254–1268.

———, Seifer, R., Baldwin, A., & Baldwin, C. (1993). Stability of intelligence from preschool to adolescence: The influence of social and family risk factors. *Child Development, 64*, 80–97.

———, Seifer, R., Barocas, R., Zax, M., & Greenspan, S. (1987). Intelligence quotient scores of 4-year-old children: Social-environmental risk factors. *Pediatrics, 79*, 343–350.

———, Seifer, R., & Zax, M. (1982). *Early development of children at risk for emotional disorder. Monographs of the Society for Research in Child Development, 47* (Serial No. 199).

Sander, L. (1975). Infant and caretaking environment: Investigation and conceptualization of adaptive behavior in a system of increasing complexity. In E. J. Anthony (Ed.), *Explorations in child psychiatry* (pp. 129–166). New York: Plenum.

Sarason, S. B. (1991). *The predictable failure of educational reform.* San Francisco: Jossey-Bass.

Schorr, L. B., Both, D., & Copple, C. (1991). *Effective services for young children.* Washington, DC: National Academy Press.

Schorr, L., & Schorr, D. (1988). *Within our reach: Breaking the cycle of disadvantage.* New York: Doubleday/Anchor.

Schweinhart, L. J., Barnes, H., & Weikart, D. P. (1993). *Significant benefits: The High/Scope Perry Preschool study through age 27.* Ypsilanti, MI: High/Scope Press.

Shade, B. J. (1982). Afro-American cognitive style: A variable in school success? *Review of Educational Research, 52,* 219–244.

Shelor, D. (1993). Bringing children to literacy through literature in primary grades. In B. Harp (Ed.), *Bringing children to literacy: Classroom at work* (pp. 1–19). Norwood, MA: Christopher-Gordon.

Shepard, L. A., & Smith, M. L. (1989). *Flunking grades: Research and policies on retention* (pp. 214–236). New York: Falmer Press.

Shiono, P. H., & Behrman, R. E. (1995). Low birth weight: Analysis and recommendations. *Future of Children, 5,* 4–18.

Singer, J. D., & Butler, J. A. (1987). The Education for Handicapped Children Act: Schools as agents of social reform. *Harvard Educational Review, 57,* 125–151.

Sirotnik, K. A. (1983). What you see is what you get—consistency, persistency, and mediocrity in classrooms. *Harvard Educational Review, 53,* 16–31.

Spencer, M. B. (1993, March). *Gender differences in neighborhood experiences and academic outcomes for urban impoverished African American youth.* Paper presented at the Biannual Meeting of the Society for Research in Child Development, New Orleans.

Sroufe, L. A. (1983). Infant-caregiver attachment and patterns of adaptation in preschool: The roots of maladaptation and competence. In M. Perlmutter (Ed.), *The Minnesota Symposium on Child Psychology, vol. 16* (pp. 41–83). Hillsdale, NJ: Erlbaum.

Sroufe, L. A. (1989). Pathways to adaptation and maladaptation: Psychopathology as developmental deviation. In D. Cicchetti (Ed.), *Rochester Symposium on Developmental Psychopathology, vol. 1, Emergence of a Discipline* (pp. 13–40). Hillsdale, NJ: Erlbaum.

————, & Fleeson, J. (1986). Attachment and the construction of relationships. In W. Hartup & Z. Rubin (Eds.), *Relationships and development* (pp.51–71). Hillsdale, NJ: Erlbaum.

————, & Rutter, M. (1984). The domain of developmental psychopathology. *Child Development, 55,* 17–29.

————, & Waters, E. (1977). Attachment as an organizational construct. *Child Development, 48,* 1184–1199.

Stedman, L. C. (1987, November). It's time we changed the effective schools formula. *Phi Delta Kappan,* pp. 215–224.

Stevenson, H. W., & Lee, S. (1990). *Contexts of achievement. Monographs of the Society for Research in Child Development, vol 55* (serial no. 221).

Strawn, J. (1992). The states and the poor: Child poverty rises as the safety net shrinks. *Social Policy Report: Society for Research in Child Development, 6*(3), pp. 1–19.

Strauss, M., Gelles, R., & Steinmetz, S. (1980). *Behind closed doors*. New York: Doubleday.

Super, C., & Harkness, S. (1986). The developmental niche: A conceptualization at the interface of child and culture. *International Journal of Behavioral Development, 9*, 545–569.

Swadener, E. B. (1989). *Children and families "at risk": Etiology, critique, and alternative paradigms*. Paper presented at the Bergamo Curriculum Theorizing Conference, Dayton, OH.

———, & Lubeck, S. (1994). *Children and families "at promise."* Albany, NY: SUNY.

Taylor, C. (1994). Assessment for measurement or standards: The peril and promise of large-scale assessment reform. *American Educational Research Journal, 31*, 231–262.

Tharp, R. G., & Gallimore, R. (1988). *Rousing minds to life*. New York: Cambridge University Press.

Thomas, A., & Grimes, J. (1995). *Best practices in school psychology-III*. Silver Spring, MD: National Association of School Psychologists.

Thompson, R. A. (1994). Emotion regulation: A theme in search of definition. In N. A. Fox (Ed.), *The development of emotion regulation: Biological and behavioral considerations. Monographs of the Society for Research in Child Development, 59* (Serial No. 240), 25–52.

Tobin, J. J. (1991, October). *Panopticism*. Paper presented at Conference on Reconceptualizing Research in Early Childhood Education, University of Wisconsin-Madison.

———. (1992). Early childhood education and the public schools: Obstacles to reconstructing a relationship. *Early Education and Development, 3*, 196–200.

Tonge, W., James, D., & Hillam, S. (1975). Families without hope. *British Journal of Psychiatry Special Publication #11*. Ashford: The Royal College of Psychiatry.

Tyack, D. (1987). Was there ever a golden age in teaching? *Harvard Educational Review, 57*, 171–186.

———, & Hansot, E. (1982). *Managers of virtue: Public school leadership in America, 1820–1980*. New York: Basic Books.

U.S. Department of Education, National Center for Education Statistics. (1993). *The condition of education, 1993*. Washington, DC: Author.

Valencia, R. (1986, November). *Minority academic underachievement: Conceptual and theoretical considerations for understanding the achievement problems of Chicano students*. Paper presented to the Chicano Faculty Seminar, Stanford University.

van IZjendoorn, M. H., Goldberg, S., Kroonenberg, P., & Frenkel, O. (1992).

The relative effects of maternal and child problems on the quality of attachment: A meta-analysis of attachment in clinical samples. *Child Development, 63,* 840–858.

———, & De Ruiter, C. (1993). Some speculations about attachment in the schools. *International Journal of Educational Research, 19,* 77–79.

Vasconcelos, T. (1995). *"Houses and fields and vineyards shall yet again be bought in this land": The story of Ana, a public kindergarten teacher in Portugal.* Unpublished doctoral dissertation, University of Illinois at Urbana-Champaign.

Verstegen, D. A. (1990). Educational fiscal policy in the Reagan administration. *Education Evaluation and Policy Analysis, 12,* 355–374.

von Bertalanffy, L. (1968). *General system theory.* New York: George Braziller.

Wachs, T.D. (1992). *The nature of nurture.* Newbury Park, CA: Sage.

Wahler, R., Leske, G., & Rogers, E. (1979). The insular family: A deviance support system for oppositional children. In L. Hamerdynck (Ed.), *Behavioral systems for the developmentally disabled, I: School and family environments.* (pp. 102–127). New York: Brunner-Mazel.

Walsh, D. J. (1989). Changes in kindergarten: Why here and now? *Early Childhood Research Quarterly, 4,* 377–391.

———. (1991). Reconstructing the Discourse on Developmental Appropriateness: A Developmental Perspective. *Early Education and Development, 2,* 109–119.

———. (1993). The defeat of literacy: Tragedy in Albemarle County. *New Advocate, 6,* 251–264.

———. (1995). *The school district that learned to talk.* Unpublished manuscript.

———, Baturka, N. L., & Smith, M. E. (1992). The two-year route to first grade: Administrative decisions and children's lives. *Educational Foundations, 6,* 67–84.

———, Baturka, N. L., Smith, M. E., & Colter, N. (1991). Changing one's mind—maintaining one's identity: A first grade teacher's story. *Teachers College Record, 93,* 73–86.

———, Davidson, J. A., Ting, H., Enos, A., & Tsai, M. (1995). *Stoney Point: Communicating at the borders.* Unpublished manuscript.

———, Ellwein, M. C., Eads, G. M., & Miller, A. K. (1991). Knocking on kindergarten's door: Who gets in? Who's kept out? *Early Childhood Research Quarterly, 6,* 89–100.

Waxman, H. C., de Felix, J. W., Anderson, J. E., & Baptiste, H. P. (1992). *Students at risk in at-risk schools.* Newbury Park, CA: Corwin.

Weissman, M. M., Leaf, P. J. & Bruse, M. L. (1987). Single parent women: A community study. *Social Psychiatry, 22,* 29–36.

Werner, E., & Smith, E. (1982). *Vulnerable but invincible.* New York: Wiley.

Wertsch, J. (1985). *Vygotsky and the social formation of mind.* Cambridge, MA: Harvard University Press.

Whelage, G.G., Rutter, R.A., Smith, G.A., Lesko, N.L., & Fernandez, R.R. (1988). *Reducing the risk: Schools as communities of support.* Madison, WI: National Center on Effective Secondary Schools.

Whitehead, B. D. (1993, April). Dan Quayle was right. *Atlantic Monthly,* pp. 47–84.

Wolf, J. (1995). *"If you haven't been there, you don't know what it's like": Life at Enchanted Gate from the inside.* Unpublished doctoral dissertation, University of Illinois at Urbana-Champaign.

Young, K. T. (1994). *Starting points: Meeting the needs of our youngest children, The report of the Carnegie Task Force on Meeting the Needs of Young Children.* New York: Carnegie Foundation.

Ysseldyke, J. E., Thurlow, M., Graden, J., Wesson, C., Algozzine, B., & Deno, S. (1983). Generalizations from five years of research on assessment and decision making: The University of Minnesota Institute. *Exceptional Education Quarterly, 4,* 75–93.

Zigler, E., & Muenchow, S. (1992). *Head Start: The inside story of America's most successful educational experiment.* New York: Basic Books.

Index

AUTHORS